Threat to Security

How Secured is India from within

Threat to Security

How Secured is India from within

P.C. Dogra, IPS (Retd.)
Ex-Director General of Police, Punjab

Foreword by
Air Chief Marshal A.Y. Tipnis, PVSM, AVSM, VM
Former Chief of the Air Staff

Manas Publications
New Delhi-110002 (INDIA)

Manas Publications
(We Convert Fighters into Writers)
(Publishers, Library Suppliers, Importers & Exporters)
4402/5-A, Ansari Road (Opp. HDFC Bank)
Darya Ganj, New Delhi-110 002 (India)
Off. 011-23260783, 23265523, Res. 011-23842660
Fax: 011-23272766
E-mail: manaspublications@gmail.com
manaspublications@yahoo.com
Website: www. manaspublications.in

2nd Impression 2015 (FP - 2007)

ISBN: 81-7049-304-8

₹ 495/-

Printed in India at
Rajdhani Printers, Delhi
and published by Mrs Suman Lata for
Manas Publications,
4402/5-A, Ansari Road, (Opp HDFC Bank),
Darya Ganj, New Delhi-110 002 (INDIA)

Foreword

Ensuring security of its territory and that of its people is the single most important function of a nation-state. Unless a nation is pro-active in fulfilling this function, other nation-states, as also non-state forces (an increasingly prominent phenomenon in recent years) will be encouraged to gnaw at the security foundations of the neglectful state. The gnawing could be emboldened into vicious biting, if not suppressed earliest. How well does India stand scrutiny against such a perception?

Very early, we as a people of an independent country, were to experience the external dimension of threats to our security. While there would be strong arguments from protagonists of the establishment for claiming reasonable adequacy of our responses to external threats, detractors could make an equally credible case insisting that we could have done better. The intention here is not to debate the point, but to make an observation that the subject of external security has been discussed in our country in the public domain for a long time, and that we have succeeded in influencing government in taking appropriate steps to ensure national security from external threats.

Could such a view be applicable to threats from within? I dare say no. The reason for this negative verdict is that there is more public ignorance than awareness of the multi-faceted dimensions of internal threats to our nationhood. While the external threat scenario far less ominous than before, internally there seems to be greater discomfiture on a number of fronts. The Indian citizen ought to be hard-questioning government on all these issues. This would be the case if we were more knowledgeable of the scourges facing us. Information through the media is not always objective or deep enough. There is a crying need for intellectuals with authoritative knowledge to disseminate the facts of the case and unravel the complexities of a specific problem and explain how the problem either is being handled or mishandled! Only through sound knowledge, study and debate can meaningful options be formulated.

Forum on Integrated National Security, presided over by Shri P.C. Dogra, has done a yeoman's service by organizing a seminar on a most relevant and contemporary topic, "How Secured is India from Within?" To examine the question, very eminent and authoritative personalities on national security were asked to speak on a number of issues concerning internal security. Each of the speakers has come forth not only with scholastic brilliance, but with hands-on practical experience, in lucidly expressing their views and offering solutions objectively. One does not necessarily have to agree with everything: but then that is the objective of a good seminar: *Initiate an intellectual debate.* For those who were not fortunate enough to hear the orations first hand, Forum on Integrated National Security have thoughtfully taken pains to collate and publish the papers. Personally I have benefited enormously by reading this volume. I recommend its reading to all those who care about India's well-being. There is every possibility that some of the observations made by the speakers/authors are found disturbing. But then reality has to be faced boldly if we have to architect a better and a more secure tomorrow for ourselves.

I congratulate Forum on Integrated National Security, in particular its President, Shri P.C. Dogra, for the success of their seminar, "How Secured is India from Within?" as also for publishing its proceedings. I wish you success in your future ventures on national security. Strategic thinking is an essential requirement of the 21st Century.

Jai Hind

A.Y. Tipnis
(Air Chief Marshall (Retd.))

Preface

A Nation is concerned about any external threat to its territorial integrity. We equip our armed forces with the state of art weapons. The state of readiness of our armed forces sends the required message to our adversary. But there has been a strategic re-orientation of the concept of national security now. Long drawn battles are ruled out. International community will intervene. There is also a nuclear thresh hold. War, its extent should be such that our adversary is not 'provoked' to unleash nuclear retaliation. Our Generals talk of short war, limited in time and space. Even that is not possible in our case with Pakistan. Stephen Cohen has said in his book *The Idea of Pakistan* that "There are senior officers who advocate "limited war" to teach Pakistan a lesson. The 2002 crisis was a turning point: Indian Generals could not promise that a limited war against Pakistan would not go "nuclear" and the political leadership concluded that the risks of such a war were too great."

Recent mobilisation of the Indian army after the terrorist attack on our Parliament on 13 Dec. 2002 and demobilisation after about eight months without engaging the enemy, under the pressure of international community clearly shows the compulsions of the Govternment of India. It has encouraged our neighbour to continue sponsoring subversive activities in our country without any let up and with impunity. But we can not go across to strike at the terrorist bases to inflict the deterrent cost on the enemy.

So it has become imperative that we give unequivocal attention to the internal security of our Nation while at the same time ensuring the inviolability and the sanctity of our borders. It is not a boundary dispute with China as it is not the Kashmir dispute with Pakistan that if and when solved will ease the border tension. It is a much bigger game of encircling India and not let it emerge as the world power.

Pak Generals feel that India was fast cracking up. Quoting Philip Cohen's book Once Again :

> For some, Kashmir is also the unraveling of India. If India gave up Kashmir, then the Indian Muslims will also come to Pakistan or would at least achieve a separate status within the restructured confederation of India. A few hard liners even look forward to the day, India might be broken up, adding to the list of independent South Asian Muslim states.

As per conservative estimates, approximately 46000 tonnes of narcotics pass through Pakistan every year. In terms of money, it generates about $ 8 billion annually. The share of ISI every year is $ 3 billion, an amount more than enough to fund the cross border terrorism. Nawaz Shrief, ex-Prime Minister of Pakistan, once told the *Washington Post* that in 1990, the then Army Chief General Aslam Beg and the ISI Chief had come out with a plan to pay for the Pakistan's covert military operations through heroin trafficking.

The presence of 15 per cent of another country's population in India underscores a strong negative impact on our national sovereignty. About fifteen to twenty million Bangladeshis have migrated to India and are illegal residents. Bangladesh has become a haven of anti-India subversive elements. ISI has set up its base here with the sole aim of breaking up North-East India. Insurgent outfits like ULFA, ATTF (All Tripura Tiger Force) and National Socialist Council of Nagaland are running business establishments in Bangladesh. Manipur is on the boil. The Meitai dominated outfits like United National Liberation Front and PREP AK want independent Manipur.

Naxalite outfits have carved out a "Compact Revolutionary Zone" comprising districts of Bihar bordering Nepal upto Rayalseema district of Andhra Pradesh. They have also formed the umbrella organisation called CCOMPOSA or Coordination Committee of Maoist Parties of South Asia from India, Nepal, Bangladesh and Sri Lanka. Lastly they met in the jungles of Dandakaranya. Maoists of Nepal and the PWG have formed Revolutionary International Movement and the bonds between Maoists-PWG and the ULFA are growing with NDFB. Kamati Pur Liberation Organisation also roped in.

According to Home Ministry information, the latest naxalite activity is spread over 125 Districts in twelve states i.e. Andhra Pradesh, Maharashtra, Orissa, Jharkhand, Madhya Pradesh, Chhattisgarh, Bihar, Uttar Pradesh, West Bengal, Tamil Nadu. Kerala and Uttranchal are the latest entries. Commenting upon the recent merger of the PWG and Maoist Communist Centre of Bihar, the report said, "It is likely to impart a qualitative impetus to naxalism that has witnessed a perceptible growth in recent years in the form of extensive militarisation, increasing violence and geographical spread."

There was major incident of arms seizure in Chittagong on April 2, 2004 in which a huge consignment of Korean, Italian, Chinese and US made weapons including 690 T56-1 Sub Machine guns, 600 T56-2 sub machine guns, 150 T-69 rocket Launchers in addition to more ancillary arms and ammunition were recovered. Jane's *Intelligence Review* has revealed that "the purchases were financed by a foreign intelligence service seeking to destablise India's North-East and that the shipment involved ULFA's military Chief Paresh Barana and NSCN's Chief Procurement Officer, Anthony Shimray.

Coming to the criminalisation of the Indian polity, N.N.Vohra Committee has observed: "The network of the mafia is virtually running a parallel Government pushing the state apparatus into irrelevance." It discloses a powerful nexus between the bureaucracy and the politicians, further with mafia gangs, smugglers and the underworld.

These are some of the disturbing issues, which have been discussed threadbare in this book. It is the publication of the *Forum on Integrated National Security* — Chandigarh. The book is the compilation of the presentations delivered in the seminar on "How Secured is India from within? Destablising Factors and Ways to Combat them", held by the Forum at Chandigarh in November 2004.

We had a tremendous response from the eminent personalities, commanding international reputation in the field of their expertise. The Forum expresses its heartfelt gratitude to them. They have been extremely kind to us. The presentations were very well written, were informative and sometimes provocative. The speakers struck a very warm and interactive chord with the audience. I am personally very grateful to these distinguished personalities who first positively responded to my request and thereafter gave a shape of an article to their views at the seminar.

I am also extremely grateful to Air Chief Marshal (Retd) A.Y. Tipnis PVSM, AVSM, VM for writing the foreword for this book. It is a great honour for the Forum. We find no words to express our gratitude. I am sure the readers will find the material in the book very absorbing and really a theme for thought.

P.C. Dogra
Chandigarh

Contents

About Our Contributors

Brahma Chellaney

A Professor of Strategic Studies at the Centre for Policy Research in New Delhi and Member of the Policy Advisory Group headed by the External Affairs Minister, Brahma Cellaney is also a newspaper columnist and television commentator. Until January 2000, Professor Chellaney was an adviser to India's National Security Council, serving as convenor of the External Security Group of the National Security Advisory Board. He was one of the authors of the Nuclear Doctrine prepared by the Board, and also played a lead role in preparing India's first-ever Strategic Defence Review as convenor of the External Security Group. He was until recently a member of the Executive Council of the Institute for Defence Studies and Analyses, New Delhi, as well as a member of the Institute's Appointments Committee. Besides, Professor Chellaney has held appointments at the Harvard University, (1987-89), the Brookings Institution (1989-91), the Johns Hopkins University's School of Advanced International Studies (1990-93), and the Australian National University (1994-96).

S.D. Muni

S.D. Muni has been Professor, Centre of South, Central, SE Asian and S-W Pacific Studies; School of International Studies and at Jawaharlal Nehru University, New Delhi, since January,

1987. He was Ambassador of India in Lao P. D.R. from November 1997 - December 1999 (on deputation from Jawaharlal Nehru University); has been a member of Official Indian delegations led by the Prime Minister and Minister of External Affairs to Nepal, Sri Lanka and Mauritius (Indian Ocean Rim Association of Regional Cooperation), during 1990-91 and 1997; also Member, National Security Council Advisory Board, 1990-91. He has been delivering annual/periodic guest lectures at professional institutions such as National Defence College, New Delhi; Higher Command Course, College of Combat, Mhow; Defence Services Staff College, Wellington (Nilgiris); Indian Military Academy, Dehradoon, and Army Medical Core Training School, Lucknow and to foreign diplomats and Foreign Service probationers at the Foreign Service Institute, New Delhi. A visiting Fellow (Strategic and Defence Studies Centre, Research School of Pacific Studies, Australian National University, Canberra, Australia, 1978-79), Founding member of Regional Centre of Strategic Studies (RCSS, Colombo); and Member of its International Research Committee 1992-99. Member of the IDSA Executive Committee, 1991-92. Parliamentary Fellow, Institute of Constitutional and Parliamentary Studies, New Delhi, 1969-70, and has authored and edited 15 books and monographs published in India and Abroad. Some of his latest publications since 2002 include : China's Strategic Engagement with the New ASEAN (Singapore, 2002), Maoist Insurgency in Nepal (Rupa, New Delhi 2003), India's Energy Security (Rupa, New Delhi 2005), and Responding to Terrorism in South Asia.

Vijay Kapoor

Vijay Kapoor, an IAS officer of 1961 batch, was a visiting fellow at Queen Elizabeth House at Oxford (UK) where he studied Development Economics. During his 35 years in the IAS, he occupied crucial positions in districts, in civic bodies and utilities and in state and federal government. From 1998-2004, he was Lieutenant Governor of Delhi, which he voluntarily vacated. As Lieutenant Governor, he was at the apex of the entire edifice of governance, civic management and development of the national capital territory of Delhi.

While in the IAS, Kapoor was Secretary in the Ministry of Defence (1992-1996), Chief Secretary of the three states of Arunachal Pradesh, Delhi and Jammu and Kashmir (1987-1992) and Chief Executive of the Municipal Corporation of Delhi and the Delhi Electricity Supply Undertaking (1983-1987). From 1977-83 he worked in the United Nations on policies concerning industry, technology and energy.

In the Ministry of Defence, Kapoor was responsible for procurement and production (through the Defence public sector undertaking as well as in cooperation with the private sector) of the entire gamut of military equipment and stores. He worked with full responsibility for interface between defence research and production.

Arun Bhagat

Arun Bhagat joining the IPS in 1961, worked as Director Intelligence Bureau, IGP Goa, Daman and Diu, and Commissioner of Police in Delhi, Director and Jt. Secretary Cabinet Secretariat, Addl. DG. CRPF, Spl. Director CBI and Director General, BSF. After retirement in 1998, he became International Consultant to UN High Commissioner of Human Rights, Geneva and National Consultant to UNDP & Consultant to Ford Foundation, was a member of 3 member committee (MHA) headed by Mr. Reberio on Police Reforms, was a member of the National Security Council Advisory Board, and regular Commentator on Radio and TV.

General V. P. Malik

General Malik was Chief of the Army Staff of the Indian Army (1997-2000), Chairman, Chiefs of Staff Committee of India from (1999-2000). As Indian Army Chief and Chairman Chiefs of Staff Committee, he planned, coordinated and oversaw execution of Operation Vijay to successfully defeat Pakistan's attempted intrusion in Kargil Sector in 1999. His tenure saw substantial enhancement of civil-military coordination in the functioning of the Government of India, and military diplomacy efforts as part of India's international relations. A graduate from the Defence Services Staff College and Madras University, General Malik is an alumnus of the National Defence College, New Delhi. He has authored several papers on defence planning and security issues and addressed many national and international seminars, civil and military institutions, universities, and industrial organisations in India and abroad. Since retirement, he keeps himself engaged in spreading awareness and sharing his views on India's national security challenges and international relations. He was a member of the National Security Advisory Board for two years. Currently, he is President of the Observer Research Foundation (ORF) Institute of Security Studies, honorary Advisor to the Centre for Policy Research, and an independent director on the board of some well-known private sector companies.

Air Marshal Vinod Patney

Commissioned into the Indian Air Force in May 1961, Vinod Patney has held the following posts in his brilliant career: Air Advisor at the High Commission of India, London; Command of a Jaguar Base; Air Officer Commanding J & K; Air Defence Commander Western Air Command; Senior Air Staff Officer, Western Air Command; Air Officer Commanding-in-Chief Central Air Command; Air Officer, Commanding-in-Chief Western Air Command (during Kargil Confict); Vice-Chief of Air Staff; has been awarded Ati Vishisht Seva Medal (1996), Param Vishisht Seva Medal (1998) and Sarvottham Yudh Seva Medal (1999), was the highest decorated serving officer in the three Armed Forces, and a member of National Security Advisory Board (2001-2004).

Lt. General Vijay Oberoi

Vijay Oberoi was commissioned in the Maratha Light Infantry in June 1961. A Graduate of the Defence Services Staff College, he later did his M.Sc. in Defence Studies from the Madras

University. He was an International fellow at the United States Army Warfare College in USA, 1988-89. Despite losing his right leg during Indo-Pak War of 1965, he soldiered on till he retired as the Vice Chief of the army staff in Sept. 2001. Before that he commanded an Armoured Division, a Strike Corps and the Training and the Western Commands. His other important appointments were Military Advisor in Malaysia and the DGMO. General Oberoi was part of the goodwill delegation in the ongoing track-II efforts to work for peace between India and Pakistan. He has recently set up the Centre for Land Warfare Studies(CLA WS), of which he is the Director. He is also the President of the War Wounded Foundation, set up to work towards meaningful rehabilitation of the war disabled.

P.C. Dogra

Sh. P.C. Dogra is a Punjab cadre IPS Officer of 1964 seniority. He is an ex-Army Emergency Commissioned Officer. After serving in various Distts as Senior Superintendent of Police, he served as D.I.G. Intelligence/CBI and in other investigating capacities. When terrorism was at its peak, he worked as D.I.G. of the two sensitive Ranges. Again on deputation to Govt. of India, he was posted as Inspector General of BSF-Jammu Frontier. Thereafter, he was in charge of IG/BSF Kashmir Frontier, IG/BSF Punjab Frontier; as Inspector General (Intelligence) at the BSF Hqrs. Delhi, where he organised anti-militancy operations in J & K; was also Addl. D.G./BSF in J & K. In the state, he worked as Director General of Police (Operations). In 1997, he took over as Director General of Police Punjab, from where he retired in 1999. He is heading the "Forum On Integrated National Security" Chandigarh which has been holding seminar (i) "Integrated Management of National Security" at Chandigarh in 2003. (ii) "How secured is India from within ? The destabilising factors and the ways to combat them" in 2004. (iii) "Foreign Policy of India and National Security" in 2005. The Forum has published a book titled, "Changing Perspective on National Security".

He has also been nominated as a Fellow of the Punjab University by the Vice-President of India.

Tarun Vijay

Tarun Vijay has been in the field of journalism since 1976; has contributed more than two thousand articles, features and interviews in various Hindi and English newspapers and magazines; was nominated on several Advisory Committees of the Govt. of India; organised the first ever-joint collaboration with Pakistan's largest circulated Urdu daily *Jang* and *Panchjanya*; was nominated as Vice-Chairman, Media Committee, Afro-Asian Games in 2001. He is a member of (i) India-China Eminent Persons Group, Ministry of External Affairs, (ii) India-Japan Eminent Persons Group, Ministry of External Affairs, (iii) Executive Committee, Editors Guild of India, SAFMA and Authors Guild of India. He has written number of books on the Cultural Heritage of India and led India's first ever Indus Expedition covering 1300 kms negotiating an altitude of 14500 feet in Ladakh region.

Abnash C. Julka

Dr. A.C. Julka is a Professor of Economics, Department of Economics, Panjab University, Chandigarh. A 'National Merit Scholar' and 'Gold Medalist', Dr. Julka received his professional training at the Panjab University, Chandigarh and Indian Statistical Institute, New Delhi. A widely travelled person, a former Chairman of the Department and Chief Editor of Social Sciences Research Journal, Professor Julka specialises in Development Economics and is a keen student of Indian Society. He has contributed extensively to professional publications and research fora.

Amarjit Singh Samra

Mr. AS Samra, former Director General of Police and Commissioner of Police (Mumbai), is the recipient of the prestigious UGC merit scholarship for post-graduate studies in Delhi and served in Maharashtra Police, Directorate of Security and Central Bureau of Investigation, he came to prominence as

Police Commissioner of Thane for maintaining peace in 1992-93. He was specially brought to Bombay as Police Commissioner to handle the communal riots. He has written a book on "The Role of Police and its Management in Modern India". He has been decorated with President Police Medal for Distinguished Service, and was selected to visit Institutions of Criminal Administration in UK and USA. Mr. Samra is working on a project to control Brand Piracy in India.

Baljit Rai

Baljit Rai joined Indian Police Service in 1954, served in composite Punjab, Delhi, Tripura, Nagaland, Rajasthan, Bihar and finally retired from service in 1986 as Director General of Police. Afterward he took to writing and brought his administrative experience to bear on the burning problems of the nation. He did extensive traveling both inside and outside of the country.

Prakash Singh

Prakash Singh was one of the most distinguished Police Officer of India and occupied highest positions in the most turbulent areas of the country; has been Director General of Border Security Force, was DGP (UP) and DGP (Assam); was awarded Padmashri for his contribution to national security. Singh has written a number of books on insurgency in Nagaland, The Naxalite Movement in India, Disaster Response in India and Kohima to Kashmir.

Brig. Kiran Krishan

Kiran Kishan an NDA alumnus and DSSC graduate, participated in the 1971 Bangladesh Liberation War; has personal experience of anti-terrorism operations; he served in the National Security Guard (NSG) during 1985-88, in the formative stages of the force. Besides establishing India's first Improvised Explosive Devices (IED) Disposal School at the NSG Training Centre,

Manesar, he had a major share in drafting (NSG's) first doctrinal pamphlet, and the country's first IED disposal manual. He has had first-hand experience of Punjab insurgency and participated in Operation Black Thunder. He commanded an engineer regiment in Jaffna (1988-90); as Commander, Faculty of NBC Protection at the CME, Pune (1991-93); and later as Deputy Director General NBC Warfare at the Army Headquarters (1997-99), worked on WMD related terrorism issues.

1

Containing The Scourge of Terrorism : The Challenges Ahead

Brahma Chellaney

Introduction

Going by the present trends, terrorism could become even a bigger scourge in the coming years without greater international cooperation and sustained anti-terror operations.

> First, the diffusion of advanced technology is facilitating acts of terror and rearing new forms of terrorism. Second, regimes that murder, maim and menace the innocent are employing export of terrorism — like classical national power projection — as an indispensable component of state power. Third, sub-state actors, some promoted by regimes and some operating with the connivance of elements within the national military, intelligence or government, will continue to employ religion or ethnic or sectarian aspirations to justify their acts of terror.

Before terrorists struck with a vengeance against the United States in September 2001, terrorism had not received serious international attention. Some Western analysts even claimed that its threat was being exaggerated. A global anti-terror campaign was long overdue, but just as a strong police and a strong military do not stop crime and aggression, this campaign does not mean that terrorism will cease to be a cost-effective political tool for those unable to deal directly with their perceived adversaries. In no other continent is the fight against terrorism and extremism more critical to international security than it is in Asia.

International Terrorism

Epicentre: After all, the epicentre of international terrorism remains in the Pakistan-Afghanistan belt. Much of Asia's terrorist violence is concentrated in its southern belt, which in the past decade emerged as the international hub of terrorism. This southern part of Asia encompassing Afghanistan, Pakistan, Uzbekistan, Tajikistan, Chinese-ruled Xinjiang and Tibet, India, Nepal, Sri Lanka, Bangladesh and Burma, is wracked by terrorist, insurgent and separatist violence in a manner unmatched elsewhere in the world. The number of annual fatalities in terrorist-related violence in southern Asia far exceeds the death toll in the Middle East, the traditional cradle of terrorism. To be sure, the entire expanse from the Middle East to Southeast Asia is home to militant groups and wracked by terrorist violence, posing a serious challenge to international and regional security.

The radicalisation of Muslims in Southeast Asia, where Islamist groups are becoming increasingly entrenched, is, however, a more recent phenomenon.

The spread of militancy and terrorism in southern Asia is linked to the Afghan war of the 1980s and the U.S. and Saudi funnelling of arms to the anti-Soviet guerrillas through Pakistan's Inter Services Intelligence (ISI) agency. The Afghan war veterans have come to haunt the security of India, Europe, the United States and several Muslim states. Many members of the Afghan war alumni returned to their homelands to wage terror campaigns against governments they viewed as tainted by Western influence. Egyptian President Anwar Sadat's assassination, for example, was linked to such inspired terror. Large portions of the multi-billion dollar military aid to the anti-Soviet Afghan rebels by the U.S. Central Intelligence Agency (CIA) was siphoned off by the conduit — the ISI — to ignite a bloody insurgency in Indian Kashmir after the agency failed to trigger an uprising in India's Punjab state despite arming Sikh dissidents.

Promoting Jihad Centre: Substantial quantities of U.S.-supplied weapons, in what was the largest covert operation in CIA's history, also found their way into the Pakistani black market, promoting a *jihad* culture within Pakistan and spreading illicit arms and militancy in a vast region stretching from Egypt to the Philippines. Afghan war veterans, or elements associated with them, were held responsible for terrorist attacks on several U.S. targets in the 1990s, including the 1998 bombings outside the American embassies in Nairobi and Dar-e-Salam, the 1996 truck bombing of the Khobar Towers, a high-rise compound that housed 2,000 American military personnel assigned to the King Abdul Aziz Airbase in Saudi Arabia, the 1995 bombing of an American-run military compound in Riyadh, the first World Trade Centre bombing in 1993, and the ambush-killing of two CIA officials outside the agency's headquarters, also in 1993.

Impact: But the greatest impact of the cross-border movement of Afghan war veterans and illegal arms was felt in southern Asia, with India bearing the brunt of the unintended consequences of the foreign interventions in Afghanistan between 1979-89. Terrorism has become a way of life in some areas of southern Asia. The only thriving democracy in this vast region is India, wedged in an arc of authoritarian or totalitarian regimes engaged in covert actions in breach of international law. These regimes either export narcotics and terrorism (Afghanistan, Pakistan and Burma) or make illicit transfers of nuclear and missile technologies (China). Pakistan indeed has been waging a war by proxy in the Indian state of Jammu and Kashmir through Islamic militants. The future of the international campaign against terrorism hinges on success in this region to root out terrorist networks and deter regimes from encouraging or harbouring armed extremists.

India, in fact, is a sort of laboratory where major acts of terror are first tried out before being replicated in other democracies in the West. The logic is that if India, the world's largest democracy, can be shaken, so can other democracies.

For example, the 1988 Panam 103 bombing replicated the mid-air bombing over the Atlantic of an Air-India commercial flight from Canada in 1985. Parallels also have emerged between the 1999 hijacking to Kandahar of Indian Airlines Flight IC-814 and the September 11, 2001, suicide hijackings, including the similar use of box-cutters and the terrorists' knowledge of cockpit systems.

India's own soft response to terrorism has emboldened international terrorists and their sponsors over the years. Pakistan has employed Afghan war veterans and its home-grown terrorists to bleed India as part of what it calls a war of "a thousand cuts." U.S. officials now acknowledge that Pakistan's "intelligence service even used Al Qaeda camps in Afghanistan to train covert operatives for use in a war of terror against India." Some *jihadis* trained by Pakistan for export to India have also turned to *jihad* against the United States. Links have emerged between the ISI and Al Qaeda terrorist network, and between Pakistani extremists and those involved in the suicide hijackings in the United States. Pakistan is home to several groups labelled "terrorist" by the U.S. government.

In fact, Pakistan remains the biggest sanctuary of Al Qaeda operatives, reinforced by Islamabad's uncanny ability to capture and deliver to the U.S. military an important Al Qaeda figure whenever it needs to deflect growing external pressure, e.g. Khalid Shaikh Mohammed, Al Qaeda's supposed third in command, who was captured by Pakistan on March 1, 2003 — just a few hours before Islamabad informed the United States that it would not be in a position to back a UN Security Council resolution in favour of the war in Iraq. Later the same month, Pakistan captured Yasser Jazeeri, another key Al Qaeda operative, to pave the way for Pakistani President Gen. Pervez Musharraf's visit to Camp David, where President George W. Bush announced a $3 billion military and economic aid package to Islamabad. Earlier, during a U.S. congressional debate on the question of foreign aid to Pakistan in March 2002, Pakistan announced the arrest of Abu Zubeida, the Al Qaeda operations chief. Then, on the eve of the first anniversary of the September 11, 2001 terrorist attacks, Pakistan arrested Ramzi Binalshib — one of the architects of those attacks — from a residential area of Karachi. Most recently, when the United States has stepped up pressure on Musharraf to allow American interrogation of Abdul Qadeer Khan, father of the Pakistani nuclear bomb, Pakistan announced the capture in May 2005 of Abu Faraj Farj, also known as Abu Faraj Libbi, another Al Qaeda commander.

India's Soft Response

Series of Mistakes: If any state strikes deals with the forces of terrorism, not only does it encourage stepped-up terrorism against its own interests, it also creates problems for other nations. A classic case is the ignominious manner India caved in on December 31, 1999, to the demands of hijackers holding a planeload of passengers aboard the Indian commercial jetliner at the terrorists' lair, Kandahar. It was a surrender unparalleled in modern world history: The Indian foreign minister personally chaperoned three jailed terrorists to freedom in a special aircraft, delivering them to their waiting comrades at Kandahar airport. This act on the New Millennium eve capped a series of mistakes in that hijacking that have exacted heavy costs.

In fact, no country could have entered the new millennium on a more ignominious note than India did. The unparalleled spectacle of the Indian foreign minister hand-delivering three freed terrorists in Kandahar ran counter not only to the fragile international consensus against surrender to terrorist demands, but also to India's own fight against international terrorism. What remains unexplained to this day is why the capitulation came with abominable grovelling.

When history is written, some blunders would stand out for the unending costs they exacted. The Kandahar capitulation on December 31, 1999, and the surrender in the Rubaiya Sayed case, exactly a decade earlier, will top the list in the post-Nehru-Indira-Rajiv period. The terrorists-for-Rubaiya Sayed swap provided Pakistan the combustible fuel it needed to trigger an insurrection in the Kashmir valley as part of what Benazir Bhutto admitted in 2003 was her government's calculated "politico-military decision to start low-intensity operations" there.

In the aftermath of the Kandahar cave-in, cross-border terrorism morphed from hit-and-run attacks to daring assaults on military camps and national emblems of power, like Parliament and Red Fort. The escalation in attacks came instantly, with the first three days of the new millennium witnessing 31 killings, including a Srinagar bombing. The hijacking of the IC-814 flight, as Strobe Talbott writes in his latest book, was "seen by many as a personal victory for Musharraf, who was widely believed to have masterminded the incident..."

Yet this architect of Kargil and the hijacking (who embraced and sheltered the three terrorists freed by India) can remain ever grateful to the Vajpayee government, which out of the blues invited him to Agra and helped make him internationally acceptable when no Western nation was willing to host him. It again came to his rescue in early 2004, beginning a new series of "peace talks" with his military regime that helped dampen international outrage over Pakistan's involvement in the worst nuclear proliferation scandal in history.

Talbott writes that when he called Jaswant Singh upon the latter's return from Kandahar, he "found him at home, sipping champagne ... He was exhausted but satisfied and convinced that he had made the right decision..." No casuistry can cloak the immense damage that decision wreaked. Saving the lives of the 161 hostages on board was important. But by the time Vajpayee invited Musharraf to Agra, two of the three freed terrorists, through their new ISI-backed terror outfits, Jaish-e-Muhammad and Al-Umar, had killed more Indians in attacks than the number of hostages for whose freedom they were released. The third freed terrorist helped finance the world's worst terrorist strikes on September 11, 2001.

For Vajpayee and company, the chickens dramatically came home to roost when evidence on the December 13, 2001, attack on Parliament revealed the involvement of one of the three terrorists air-delivered in Kandahar — Masood Azhar and his Jaish-e-Muhammad. India then spent hundreds of millions of dollars in a 10-month long mobilisation of the Indian military for a war Vajpayee never intended to wage. Scores of Indian military men were killed in mine-related and other accidents during this empty display of force. The Kandahar costs will remain incalculable.

The story behind Jaswant Singh's wacky flight to known terrorist territory is no less bizarre. It began with the airing of his hallucinations. No sooner had the hijacked jetliner landed in Kandahar than the foreign minister briefed newspaper editors on the golden opportunity it presented to drive a wedge between the Taliban and its sponsor, Pakistan! Those published accounts showed the make-believe world in which he existed. Preparations to cave in had begun days before the actual capitulation, with security agencies, on political direction, aiding demonstrations by hostages' relatives, including by identifying the locations of the crisis-group meetings. Later, television networks were disingenuously blamed for having built up undue public pressure through their coverage of those protests.

Years later, several troubling questions remain, even as the nation has forgotten the brave young hostage whose throat was fatally slit, halal-style, for resisting the hijackers. Another society would have immortalised him as a hero. No explanation was ever offered for the fiasco at Amritsar airport because of which the commandeered plane took off for Lahore, where the hijackers (armed until then with box-cutters) received pistols. Why didn't anyone on the ground shoot and puncture the plane's tyres? Despite a trumpeted enquiry, no one has been punished because confusion had reigned at the very top in New Delhi. Clumsily, India ended up negotiating on bended knees.

Vajpayee has never answered the central question that even if India had been left with no choice but to give in to the hostage-takers' demand, why did the foreign minister travel to the terrorist retreat of Kandahar to hand-deliver, not wailing babies, but inveterate fiends with known Al Qaeda and ISI links. Surely, the hijackers and their masters had not demanded that India bring public shame to itself by turning its foreign minister into a terrorist chaperon. The widely-published photograph of a beaming Jaswant Singh at Kandahar airport walking hand-in-hand with the thuggish Taliban's foreign minister, now rotting in

US custody, conflicts with what his friend Talbott quotes him as saying: "He had been lucky to get out of there alive".

Jaswant Singh went to Kandahar with premeditation. At the Cabinet Committee on Security (CSS) meeting on the morning of December 31, 1999, when Jaswant Singh announced that he was flying to Kandahar with the three terrorists, L.K. Advani questioned the move. Vajpayee's telltale silence, however, left no one in doubt that he had cleared Jaswant Singh's terrorist handover. Yet, weeks later, the same Vajpayee put his foot down firmly when his foreign minister sought to compound the infamy by sending a cheque of 1.12 lakh dollars to the Taliban for "services" rendered at Kandahar.

In power, with courtiers galore and a toadying media, Vajpayee found virtue in being enigmatic, ambiguous and unfathomable. Taking flattery over his poetry to heart, he versed, parsed and spun his words to meet different situations. Today, bereft of the trappings of power, Vajpayee needs to answer that gnawing question on Kandahar: *When India had to bend, why did it crawl?*

> *Several larger questions also arise:*
>
> Has India learned any lesson from Kandahar, in keeping with the saying, 'When you lose, don't lose the lesson'?
>
> Will India be able to handle the next big hostage crisis more professionally?
>
> No Americans have been killed by terrorists in the US since after 9/11 because the US military has gone after terrorists overseas, despite the Iraq invasion serving as a recruiting boon to the Al Qaeda.
>
> India, in contrast, has suffered its biggest terrorist strikes since 9/11.
>
> Does India have any strategy to counter threats from qualitatively escalating international terrorism, other than 'talking peace' with terrorist-patron Pakistan?

Terrorists see India as a soft target because it imposes no costs on them and their sponsors. Although the problem of terrorism in India has been building up since the 1980s, successive

Indian governments have done little to combat it through a prudent strategy backed by firm resolve. Terrorism has been treated largely as a law-and-order issue. Each time there is a major terrorist attack in any area, the Central Government promises to send more security forces there. To treat terrorism essentially as a law-and-order problem is to do what the terrorists want—sap your strength. No amount of security can stop terrorism if the nation is reluctant to go after terrorist cells and networks and those that harbour terrorists.

Terrorist forces grievously miscalculated that if India can bow, they could also tame the United States, the most powerful democracy. America responded to the suicide hijackings by declaring its own *jihad* on the *jihadis*. India, in contrast, stands out for its reluctance to fight its own war against terrorism and for having invited expanded terrorism through its past compromises with terrorists.

Looking Ahead

Misconception: Due to the largely misconceived U.S. invasion of Iraq, the U.S.-led global war on terror now stands derailed, even as the scourge of terrorism has spread to more nations. The U.S. occupation of Iraq has proved divisive in international relations, splitting the world and fracturing the global consensus to fight terror. Instead of targeting terrorist cells and networks wherever they exist, President Bush has been compelled by critics at home and abroad to justify his invasion of Iraq. In the process, it has been virtually forgotten that the September 11, 2001 terrorist attacks happened not because of Iraq but because of the terrorist nurseries in the Afghanistan-Pakistan belt. In fact, by speciously linking Iraq with the Al Qaeda to justify its invasion, Washington created a self-fulfilling prophesy that now haunts it.

The Iraq mess has discredited Bush's doctrine of pre-emption, weakening his hand against North Korea. Bush showed that while the sole superpower can do as it pleases, it can neither pre-empt chaos nor win peace. American 'soft power' has been a major casualty of the Iraq occupation, which has helped portray the United States as ham-fisted and unconcerned about the opinions of other states.

Contradictary Approach: Moreover, the contradictions in Bush's own approach have come to the fore. Take for instance his accent on promoting democracy in Iraq while shoring up a military dictatorship in Pakistan and shying away from direct elections in Iraq itself. Or the way he invaded Iraq to eliminate Weapons of Mass Destruction (WMD) that were not there but has now allowed Pakistan, with real WMD, to escape international censure for selling nuclear secrets to three other renegade nations — North Korea, Iran and Libya.

The reality is that international terrorism threatens the very existence of democratic, secular states. Regrettably, the Iraq occupation has not only aggravated a Muslim-Christian divide in the world, it has also given a new lease of life to the Al Qaeda by handing it a fresh cause. It is time that the anti-terror war was brought back on course through renewed international consensus.

The Need for International Cooperation

Terrorism is the cowards' weapon, as it involves sneakiness and obviates facing an enemy. The only defence against the sly, murderous terrorists is offence aimed at hounding, disrupting, and smashing their cells, networks, and safe havens. Against covert, unconventional aggression, counteraction must also employ clandestine, unconventional methods in order to strike at the heart of a terrorist group and disrupt its cohesion, credibility, and operational capacity. Never before has there been a greater need for close international cooperation on intelligence and law enforcement, especially because of the stateless nature of some terrorists. However, no terrorist group can train and plan a major action, such as the kamikaze style strikes against the United States in September 2001 or the 1993 Bombay bombings or the December 2001 attack on the Indian Parliament, without sanctuary provided by a nation-state. The war on terrorism has to extend to the known sanctuaries of international extremists. It is laughable that a major terrorist sanctuary like Pakistan is presented as an ally in the war on terror, simply because its military ruler has become America's pet dictator.

More broadly, it will require a sustained campaign to eliminate the forces of *jihad* that pursue violence as a sanctified tool of religion and a path to redemption. The challenge is also broad: The entire expanse from the Middle East to Southeast Asia is home to militant groups and troubled by terrorist violence, posing a serious challenge to international and regional security. As terrorist bombings in several nations show, any nation can become a target.

The terror attacks since 9/11 signal the new face of terrorism: Indiscriminate, large-scale killing of civilians to achieve an absolute victory of radical Islam over the West. This is very different from the objectives of the traditional terrorists, such as those in Northern Ireland, Sri Lanka and Spain's Basque region, for whom selective use of terror has been a means to strengthen their negotiating leverage and advance ethnic or sectarian interests.

Battling the new breed of terrorists would require varying, *ad hoc* political coalitions in the world. The scourge of transnational terrorism, however, cannot be stemmed if attempts are made to draw distinctions between good and bad terrorists, and between those who threaten their security and those who threaten ours. The viper reared against one target-state is a viper against another or against oneself. For example, the Taliban and the anti-India extremists trained and armed by Islamabad have come to haunt Pakistan's own security. U.S. policy-makers in hindsight must regret some of their past actions in Afghanistan and Pakistan.

Prodded by the intense lobbying of the U.S. firm, Unocol, which sought to build oil and gas pipelines from Turkmenistan to Pakistan and India via Afghanistan, the Clinton administration acquiesced in the Taliban's rise to power. Even after the thuggish militia let loose a reign of terror in Kabul, carrying out summary executions, banishing women from the work-force and forcibly herding men into mosques for prayers, the U.S. State Department publicly hoped the new situation presented "an opportunity for a process of national reconciliation to begin." Fattened by soaring profits from heroin trade, the Taliban, in alliance with Pakistani intelligence, fostered narco-terrorism and swelled the ranks of the Afghan war alumni waging transnational terrorism. The ISI, with its continuing addiction to drug trafficking and terrorism, has found it difficult to kick its old habits.

The United States has to ensure that it does not repeat the very mistakes of the past that have come to trouble its security and that of the rest of the free world. The security of the United States and other secular, democratic societies is interconnected. The war against terrorism is essentially to protect the freedoms and tolerant spirit of pluralistic societies.

To help reclaim the global fight against terror, the United States needs to learn the lessons from its past policies that gave rise to the Frankensteins like Osama bin Laden, Mullah Mohammed Omar and Saddam Hussein. Even if bin Laden is captured, his seizure — like that of Saddam — is unlikely to provide a respite.

First is the need to keep the focus on longer-term goals and not be carried away by political expediency and narrow military objectives. By focusing on immediate goals, U.S. policy-makers in the past ended up creating monsters that they now have to fight. The Reagan Doctrine of arming anti-communist "freedom fighters" in places such as Afghanistan, Angola, Cambodia and Nicaragua put an ideological stamp on a strategic-policy shift that defined Third World insurgencies and revolutionary governments as the source of the most serious 'future security threats' to the United States. That new emphasis gave birth to the doctrine of *low-intensity conflict*, or LIC.

By funnelling billions of dollars worth of arms, including sophisticated surface-to-air missiles, tanks and howitzer guns, through conduit States and their agencies, the United States allowed the latter to bring in their own interests, biases and rivalries into play. Pakistan, for example, used its participation in America's largest covert operation not so much to rout the Soviet forces in Afghanistan as to strengthen its military position against India and to favour Afghan guerrilla groups based in its Peshawar city (such as Gulbuddin Hekmatyar's Hezbul-e-Islami) rather than assist groups engaged in active combat inside Afghanistan. Pakistan could push its own agenda because the United States accepted its condition that the ISI agency organises the weapons flow and pinpoint the arms recipients. However, as two American scholars, Lucy J. Mathiak and Lora Lumpe, have written, the "*ISI appropriated for its own purposes an estimated 50% to 70% of the military resources intended for the mujahideen ... The diversions were known at the time within the region and within the United States but were accepted as an unpleasant but necessary element of the aid program without an alternative conduit for aid.*"

It was thus no surprise that such large-scale, indiscriminate flow of arms, with little oversight over where the weapons were going and little thought being given to the long-term consequences, destabilised the affected regions (including southern Asia but particularly Pakistan) and created the Frankensteins that have come to haunt Western security. Hekmatyar, fattened by the ISI at the expense of U.S. taxpayers, was responsible more than anyone else in blocking a peaceful transition to post-Soviet rule in Afghanistan. Another Frankenstein, Osama bin Laden, was unsuspectingly endorsed by the CIA during the 1980s Afghan war. And in response to his subsequent terrorist exploits of the 1990s, Washington has done precisely what bin Laden himself did — it "mythologised him," turning him into a hero for Muslim radicals across the globe. It was at a White House ceremony attended by some turbaned and bearded 'holy warriors' from Afghanistan in the mid-1980s that President Ronald Reagan proclaimed *mujahideen* like bin Laden as the "moral equivalent of the Founding Fathers" of the United States. One such "moral equivalent of the Founding Fathers," Mullah Mohammad Omar, the one-eyed Taliban chief, gave vent to his destructive genius in spring 2001 by demolishing Afghanistan's most famous antiquities, including two towering, 1,500-old Buddhas carved into a sandstone cliff at Bamiyan—the priceless legacy of Indian Buddhist pilgrims who settled in the region before the advent of Islam.

The *second* lesson is that the problem of and solution to terrorism are linked. Terrorism not only threatens the free, secular world but also springs from the rejection of democracy and secularism. The terrorism-breeding swamps can never be fully drained as long as the societies that rear or tolerate them are not de-radicalised and democratised. It has become fashionable to state that war makes strange bedfellows and, therefore, it makes sense for the United States to line up in the anti-terror campaign even unsavoury allies—regimes that bankroll militant Islamic fundamentalism overseas, such as those of Saudi Arabia and the United Arab Emirates; the tyrannical Central Asian autocracies run by Soviet hold overs; and military-ruled, terrorism-exporting Pakistan.

> After all, to get rid of Nazism, the allies needed Stalin. But Stalin didn't create Hitler or foster Nazism; nor was Stalin's removal necessary to eradicate Nazism. The anti-terror war can succeed only through the reform of states that directly or indirectly contribute to the rise of virulent Islamic fundamentalism extolling violence as a sanctified religious tool.

Saudi Arabia, with its one-century-old political tradition of Wahhabi Islam, practices the fringe form of Islamic extremism that President Bush says he is targeting. Pakistan, too, is heavily under the influence of the Wahhabi religious movement, the source of modern Islamic extremism. So critical Saudi Arabia has been to regional U.S. policy initiatives that at no time did Washington seek to restrain its cloistered rulers from funding the establishment of Muslim extremist groups and *madrasas*, the religious schools that prepare tomorrow's holy warriors. From Africa to Southeast Asia, Saudi petrodollars have played a key role in fomenting militant Islamic fundamentalism that regards the West, Israel and India as its enemies. Only after the role of Saudi suicide hijackers came to light, has realisation dawned about the thin line separating philanthropy and advocacy of militant fundamentalism.

The military objectives of the anti-terror campaign are far easier to accomplish than the political goal to ensure that societies do not promote, shelter or condone terrorists. The most daunting task would be to inculcate a secular and democratic ethos in societies steeped in religious and political bigotry. Scoring any enduring success in the political anti-terror campaign will take time, requiring perseverance and long-term strategic engagement.

The political campaign has to ensure that nations do not fund terrorists, or terrorist prep schools, or religious bodies that spew poison; that they do not train, arm or harbour terrorists; and that they do not serve as channels for money-laundering. If destroying the Taliban has proved difficult, imagine what it will take to politically dismantle the Taliban's cradle – the terrorist infrastructure in Pakistan, including the *madrasas* that are training tomorrow's bin Ladens. Equally challenging would be to dissuade Pakistan from continuing to send covert operatives into India to wage *jihad.* The terrorists who pursue *jihad* make little distinction between the United States, Israel and India.

A *third* lesson to heed is not to turn the war against terrorism into an ideological battle to self-serve one's strategic interests. The dangers of adding religious overtones to the fight have been understood well, but not the perils of putting an ideological gloss to it. The first war of the 21st century is already being likened to the last war of the 20th century –– the fight against communism — with some U.S. commentators suggesting that it will take a new cold war to defeat terrorism.

From spearheading the fight against communism to leading the war on terrorism, the United States has come full circle. About five decades after President Truman declared America was in war to protect freedom from communism, Bush proclaimed it is in war to defend freedom from terrorism. The cold-war emphasis on 'containment' of communism finds its echo in the new stress on containment of terrorism. And just as human rights and democracy become *secondary* to the cold-war imperative of roping in allies, however dictatorial their political set up, there is similar indifference to the record of the new-war partners. It should, however, not be forgotten that terrorism springs from religious extremism, which in turn flows from the rejection of secularism and abrogation of human rights. Democratic societies in general do not breed and shelter international terrorists.

Terrorism can be stemmed only through concerted, sustained international effort, not by employing cold war-style methods. In any case, the cold war was won by the West not so much by military means as by spreading market capitalism to other regions that "*helped suck the lifeblood out of communism's global appeal,*" making it incapable of meeting the widespread yearning for a better life. Not only does a new cold war not fit well with the interests of the only superpower on the world stage, it could also prolong the fight against terrorism by deepening the problem. Rather than make the fight divisive, the international consensus on battling terrorism should be preserved and strengthened. This is especially so because critics charge that the United States, having been born in war and having waged war ever since, was uncomfortable without a foe since the end of the cold war — that is, it was in search of an enemy. Now that America has a resilient foe to battle — another 'ism' — it should behave as the leader of the world, not of one camp or as a self-absorbed bully. The outcome of this war will determine the security of all free societies. But in the interim, the world, disturbingly, seems to be becoming harder, fiercer and less tolerant.

2

North-East Insurgencies: The External Dimension

S.D.Muni

Introduction

The North-East region of India has been a chronic victim of festering insurgencies. India's security forces are confronting this challenge to internal security for a long time without much success. There are obvious internal roots of these insurgencies as well as the powerful external dimension that keep the fires burning in this sensitive region. Several scholarly studies have been published to understand the complexity of the challenge and help evolve effective policy guidelines. In this presentation, the focus will be only on the external dimension which needs a constant review and re-assessment in respect of the changing dynamics of India's relations with the immediate neighbours that share border with the turbulent North-East region. However, before coming to this external dimension, it is necessary to keep in mind a broad profile of the region. This brings to the fore three aspects of the insurgency-infected region that needs to be underlined.

Ethnic Diversity

One is the tremendous ethnic diversity of the region. There are about 200 tribes living in the region with most having a rich cultural tradition, and alloyed with a strong historical perception. The numerical strength of these tribes is not a major factor as none of the tribes is larger than 2 million in number. These smaller groups are struggling for their own identity in terms of their cultural heritage which is causing a lot of problems both between the tribal groups as also between each one of them and the larger Indian national identity.

The character of insurgencies, therefore, is primarily ethnic, not to be confused or linked with the left extremism quite rampant in the nearby regions of West Bengal, Orissa, Bihar and Jharkhand. *Secondly,* this is an area which is most underdeveloped. It has remained, administratively and economically neglected not only for the past nearly sixty years of India's independence but also even during the British period. The Colonial administration was adequately pre-occupied with their exploitation of the Indian heartland without seeing much advantage in developing this region. The British found that the revenue which they could earn from this region would not be able to meet with the administrative expenditure required to effectively govern the area. Accordingly, for them, the best way was to leave the people of Northeast on their own.

The governments of independent India followed the overall strategy of their Colonial masters not realising that the ungoverned, un-administered and underdeveloped people will eventually be pushed into political revolt. The proximity of the region to China might have added strategic consideration to India's policy-makers that its underdevelopment and inaccessibility would deter the Chinese from advancing southwards. The democratic imperative of Indian polity with only a tiny presence of representatives of this region in Parliament has also added to the neglect of this region all these years. The British by being neglectful, had also reinforced the sense and search of independence of these people which came to be expressed in terms of separatist demands reinforced by developmental neglect. No wonder, most of the insurgencies have the separatist character now.

Geo-Strategic Composition and Location

The *third* aspect, in addition to these two characterstics of region of ethnic diversity and under-development, that needs to be paid attention is the geo-strategic composition and location of the Northeast region. Geographically, the Northeast is landlocked, nay externally locked. The geographical link between this region and the Indian mainland is thin exceedingly and most vulnerable, through the "chicken's neck" as is popularly known. In contrast to this link, the Northeast shares large borders with the foreign countries Nepal, Bhutan, China, Myanmar, Bangladesh (erstwhile east-Pakistan). The Northeast, along with some of these neighbouring countries like Nepal and Bhutan, has no direct access to sea. The geo-strategic location of the Northeast poses a challenge in itself due to the nature of India's relationship with each of these neighbours. Except for Bhutan, most of these neighbours have been either hostile or indifferent to India's security sensitivities including those arising out of the insurgencies in Northeast.

In a broader sense, the external aspect of the Northeast's geo-strategic location deserves to be seen beyond its immediate neighbourhood. The whole of ASEAN has to be taken into account because one of the ASEAN member, Myanmar shares direct border with the region but its other members, like Thailand and the whole of the former Indo-China region have linkages of cultural identity and economic promise, as below. Culturally, the West is also present in the Northeast in the form of a strong Missionary influence. As a result of the presence of the Christian Missionaries, and the proximity of the region to China, the West has always shown considerable interest in India's Northeast, particularly during the Cold war years. One wonders if the Purulia airdrop of arms was a crude reflection of this interest in the area.

It is due to the combination of the three factors of ethnic diversity, under-development and externally locked geo-strategic location, that the challenge of insurgency in the region has been a formidable one. The lack of a comprehensive assessment of these three characteristics has exposed India's weakness in her political, administrative and security responses to insurgency all these years. Unless there is a well thought-out strategy that is based on a balanced assessment of all the three characteristics, the challenge of the Northeast will not be effectively met. Since the concern here is with the external dimension, consideration is aimed at its various imperatives.

External Dimension—The Negative Implications

The Northeast's external dimension is both a liability as well as an asset towards resolving the insurgency challenge in the region. As a liability, there have been five areas of concern. *First* has been the exploitation of the insurgencies and the resulting internal conflict in this region by the interested immediate neighbours. During the sixties and the seventies, both China and Pakistan exploited the insurgencies to keep India weakened and on defence. There are reliable accounts that Pakistan's military intelligence agencies like the ISI had started fishing into India's troubled Northeast by the mid-sixties by supplying arms to Naga and ULFA insurgents among other groups.

China had also supported the insurgencies to keep India internally weak and engaged as a part of its conscious and calculated policy, at least until the eighties. China has since distanced itself from any active involvement with the Northeast insurgents, though the possibility of some of these groups occasionally seeking shelter in Chinese territory without the official blessings may not be ruled out. In view of the positive turn in Sino-Indian relations and also in view of a definite shift in China's approach towards the revolutionary and insurgent groups in the neighbouring Asian countries, it may be hoped that there would be no Chinese support to Northeast insurgent movements at least overtly.

India hoped that after the emergence of Bangladesh, Pakistani interference in the Northeast would be contained, but unfortunately, since the takeover of the army in Bangladesh in a bloody coup in 1975, India's worries on this count have not disappeared. Not so even after the restoration of democratic order in 1990-91. In fact at one stage, the BNP leader and

Prime Minister Begum Khalida Zia went to the extent of describing the Northeast insurgents as freedom fighters. The influence of Pakistani military and intelligence agencies reportedly persists in Bangladesh and many of the Northeast insurgents leaders have made Bangladesh as safe havens for their violent operations in India. The Indian government has repeatedly drawn Bangladesh government's attention to this aspect, with detailed accounts of training camps and insurgent leaders' financial and political stakes in Bangladesh, with the help and connivance of the government in Dhaka, but to no avail.

Besides Bangladesh, there were also instances of Nepal doing its bit in supporting the ULFA uprising and other Northeast insurgencies during the late sixties and early seventies when Indo-Nepal relations were passing through difficult times. Nepal also remained active in this respect during the Sikkim movement during 1974-75, that eventually culminated in Sikkim's integration with India, a development that Nepal's Monarchy had viewed with considerable concern. The insurgent groups have also sought shelter and sanctuaries in Bhutan's eastern flank, taking advantage of its dense forest and difficult terrain. There were even reports of Bhutanese softness towards these groups, largely due to its own concerns of internal security. But it would be unfair to see any Bhutanese connivance and support to the insurgents. This was amply demonstrated in Bhutanese operations to flush these groups out of the Bhutanese territory in December 2003. The cooperation extended by Bhutan was appreciated by the then Indian Prime Minister Vajpayee even at the SAARC summit in Islamabad in January 2004.

Neighbouring countries like Bangladesh and Nepal have added to the Northeast insurgency in a different way also. The illegal migrations from Bangladesh and the settlement of Nepalese in the Northeast both of Indian Nepalese (from Darjeeling and Sikkim regions) and those from Nepal (coming to India under 1950 Treaty in search of economic opportunities) have complicated identity issue of the Northeast tribal groups like ULFA and BODO. These groups have initially reacted against the presence of "foreigners" in their region, as these outsiders have cornered their jobs and economic opportunities. The influx of illegal immigrants from Bangladesh is also changing the demographic composition of some of the Northeastern states as the number of Muslims is rising, threatening the cultural composition of traditional people.

Closely linked with the conscious and calculated support of some of the neighbouring countries at various time spans to the Northeast insurgencies is the supply of arms to them through these countries. We mentioned about the "Purulia arms drop" master minded by the West-based underworld of arms supplies to this region. Arms, as noted earlier have also been supplied to the insurgent groups by the ISI and such other forces hostile to India's security. In 2004, a massive arms supply chain was unearthed through Bangladesh's Chittagong and Cox's Bazzar ports in the extreme southeast access to the Indian Ocean. India's request to Bangladesh to jointly investigate this chain, or atleast take India into confidence in such investigations were not responded to favourably by the Khalida Zia government.

Suspicion is rife in concerned circles that well placed BNP supporters were involved in these illegal lethal operations. It is believed that the underworld arms network that operate through Thailand or Singapore have been active in this regard. There are also reports of the surplus of Vietnam and Cambodian conflict weapons being sold to these insurgent groups through such covert networks. The possibility of arms being supplied to the Northeast insurgents through the Burmese ethnic warlords and Yunnan based underworld arms and drugs mafia have also been indicated in media reports on many occasions.

The Northeast insurgents have networked with each other as also with the similar insurgent groups in the neighbouring countries. The reports of Nepal Maoists having links with the ULFA, BODO and the KLO (Kamtapur Liberation Organisation) have been widely circulated. As with the Nepal Maoists such links are, however, non-ideological. While the Maoists are fighting for restructuring Nepal's feudal order, the Northeast insurgents, as discussed earlier, are waging identity wars to seek separation and/or greater autonomy. The links between them are therefore operational and logistic in nature, aimed at arms procurement, training, sanctuaries and medical support, drug and money transactions etc. It is necessary to understand this difference in drafting any approach to dealing with these insurgencies. The other type of cross-border link between one and another insurgent group could also be ethnicity based.

It is known fact that the Naga community is divided between India and Myanmar and it is natural for the Naga groups across the border to seek support and sustenance from each other. The Naga groups had also established operational links with the Karan National Army of Myanmar. The tendency among the insurgent groups is that in their respective fights against the State, either Indian or in the neighbouring country, they see a common enemy and coordinate their operations to deal with this common enemy. The important point that deserves to be underlined in this respect is that while the insurgent groups have effectively networked with each other to enhance their mutual cooperation against the South Asian States, the latter mostly work at cross-purposes with each other on the serious question of internal security.

External Dimension : The Cooperative Potential

The real policy question is how can India deal with the negative implications of the external dimension to the Northeast insurgency? There are obviously two ways to proceed with it. One is multilateral and the other one is bilateral. Multilaterally all these countries neighbouring the Northeast are members, collectively or differently, of three multilateral cooperative organizations namely; SAARC (South Asian Association For Regional Cooperation), BIMSTEC (Bay of Bengal Multi-Sectoral Technical and Economic Cooperation) and ASEAN (Association of Southeast Asian Nations), along with India. All the three organisations have adopted commitment to fight terrorism; SAARC since 1987 and ASEAN and BIMSTEC since 2003 and 2004 respectively. In fact, SAARC's concern to fight terrorism predates the post 9/11 global concern in this regard by nearly fifteen years. At the very first SAARC summit, concern to fight against the menace of terrorism at the regional level was voiced in 1985 and the regional Convention to that effect was adopted in 1987.

However, the commitment enshrined in the Convention was not adhered to seriously by many of the signatory countries. How could they if some of them like Bangladesh and Pakistan had a conscious policy to encourage cross-border terrorism against India. The excuse to avoid implementation was rationalised under the cover of one of the provisions of the 1987 Convention which said that enabling national laws will have to be enacted to carry out the commitment. Some of the countries did not ratify the Convention nor did they adopt enabling legislation for want of political will. Now in the context of the post 9/11 developments and under the thrust of the US led "war against global terrorism", attention on the ineffectiveness of the SAARC Convention against terrorism has been refocused. As a result, the Kathmandu SAARC Summit in 2002 decided to revamp the Convention and a committee has been set up to look into its legal and administrative aspects.

Objectively speaking, this re-look on the SAARC Convention has been forced by the international pressures where the US is fighting terrorist in Pakistan. There has also been the United Nations Resolution No.1723, adopted after 9/11 under the US pressure. But unless there is a change in the political will among SAARC countries, nothing much could be achieved. There are hopes that with the growing terrorist challenge within Pakistan–recall the attacks on General Musharraf's life–and now also in Bangladesh, matters may improve. But this is only a faint hope as yet.

So far as BIMSTEC and ASEAN are concerned, their commitments to fight terrorism are entirely post-9/11. And this commitment, at least in ASEAN, is primarily defined in terms of the priorities of the "global war against terrorism" with its implicit bias against *jehadi terrorism*. Accordingly, its relevance to the South Asian situation, and in India's Northeast is limited, because insurgencies and terrorism in South Asia are far more diversified and complex than the *jehadi terrorism*. Nonetheless, the significance of the regional commitments cannot be under estimated since this has created the correct regional atmosphere to deal with the forces of instability and insecurity. The efforts under these commitments may be made to curb the flow of arms and money through under world networks from and through the ASEAN and BIMSTEC regions into India's Northeast. There may also be efforts to share and coordinate intelligence and put pressure on any defiant member of the organisation to render necessary help. All this is helpful, though may not prove to be *panacea* for India's worries and concerns. In any case, multilateral arrangements in dealing with specific problems of internal security always have inbuilt structural constraints.

This brings forth the bilateral aspect of cooperation between India and its neighbours to help deal with the Northeast insurgencies. The example of cooperation between India and Bhutan, through coordinated action against the ULFAs, BODOs and the KLO was mentioned earlier. This coordinated action had come after much hesitation and preparation on the part of Bhutan. The insurgent camps in Bhutanese territories not only had created internal security problems for Bhutan but there were constraints on the small Bhutanese security forces to deal with these insurgent sanctuaries. There are still persisting questions about the fallout of these operations on the residual nature of the problem. Confusion lingers on the total strength of the insurgents that were flushed out of their sanctuaries in Bhutan and where did they go. How will Bhutan be made secure from any such sanctuaries in future if the insurgents decide to slip into Bhutan again? Has Bhutanese action sufficiently crippled the strength of the insurgents or they have just relocated themselves?

Operation Golden Bird: The other country that also bilaterally helped India in dealing with the Northeast insurgents was Myanmar. In 1995, after visits of Indian Army Chief, co-ordinated operations were undertaken in 1995 in the name of "Operation Golden Bird" which put considerable pressure on the Naga groups. Again in 2003, some of the camps of the Khaplang group were completely destroyed by the Myanmarese forces on the basis of intelligence provided and requests made by the Indian side. The question of cooperation in dealing with the insurgency problem at the bilateral level was raised by India during the visit of Myanmar's military ruler, General Than Swae in 2004.

While assurance of cooperation were extended by the Myanmarese guest, there are obvious reservations on their part to carry out Bhutan like operations. India has also been pleading with Bangladesh for bilateral cooperation in dealing with the issue of cross-border insurgencies but as noted earlier, Bangladesh is not forthcoming at all. Some degree of bilateral cooperation is also evident between India and Nepal, but not to the extent where both the sides are satisfied with each other's effective action. The nature and content of bilateral cooperation in dealing with the problems on internal insecurity naturally depends upon the texture of bilateral political relations. If these relations are not very harmonious, not much cooperation can be expected.

Appraisal

The question of multilateral and bilateral cooperation with India's neighbours in dealing with the Northeast insurgency should not be seen in the context of security issues alone. The problems of insurgencies are not simply law and order problems nor are they the issues of terrorism as understood generally in the post 9/11 context. These are socio-economic and cultural problems and unless the basic faultlines are addressed, one cannot find viable solutions to these challenges. It is necessary for India to address the developmental question of the Northeast in its approach to its neighbours. SAARC, ASEAN and BIMSTEC must be given momentum as development organisations and the cooperative fallout of this momentum would positively impinge on the socio-economic challenges of the Northeast.

There is something in the Chinese approach in this respect that India can draw lessons from. The Yunnan province of China is somewhat similarly landlocked and geo-strategically located in relations to China's neighbours. China has pursued a systematic economic engagement with its immediate Southern neighbours like Myanmar, Laos, Thailand and Vietnam to help Yunnan open up economically. One of the important considerations behind China's cooperation with Pakistan and now with India is to open up its under-developed western region. India has to pursue a vigorous "Look-east" policy and SAARC cooperation keeping in mind the developmental imperative of the Northeast.

Northeast can develop faster and moderate its insurgencies by getting economically and culturally integrated not only with India but also with the border areas of its neighbouring countries. Opening and encouraging border trade with China and Myanmar and strengthening cooperation with Bangladesh, Bhutan and Nepal will greatly help India's Northeast fulfill its economic aspirations. What is needed is a rapid laying down of developmental infrastructure in the Northeast and building its connectivity, through rail, road, air and communication linkup, with the neighbouring countries. This will also help the Northeast integrate itself internally, and also with the Indian heartland. For a long-term strategy, law and order approach will have to be pursued along with developmental incentives and political accommodation.

3

Good Governance — Key to Stability and Economic Development of the Nation

Vijay Kapoor

Other than organising the kind of interaction as of now and that of the last year through seminars, it is crystal clear that there are two aspects in which the forum could play a role in generating informed discussion on security related issues. First, it is to generate enough information to which general public would have access. There is a widely expereinced feeling of paucity of information — apart from its being difficult to access — on issues of national concern among not only common citizens, but also scholars. I am saying this because it is after spending about 43 years in government that I am now experiencing the paucity of information experienced by common citizen. I don't know why it is so in this country which has a tradition of openness.

I came across a book written by a Pakistani journalist who is less than 30 years old, who has visited various parts of Pakistan, gone to various districts, visited training camps and other headquarters of various Tanzeems and then has documented the whole information. The book does not contain much of analysis but it does contain loads of information. It has lists of all *Madarsas*, list of training camps, list of various Tanzeems. It catalogues the important people in those places, their sources of funding, their activities. I have not come across information of this type published in India. Recently, I saw a not very well known Pakistani journal which had an article about the resurgence of militancy in Baluchistan that had shown signs of weakening in the past years. But it is now showing resurgence. I was amazed to see the amount of information contained in that article, not much of analyses again. But it gave a complete catalogue of incidents from 1st January 2004 in the entire Baluchistan — and it contained dates of occurrence, places of occurrence and facts about the incidents that had happened. I have not been able to lay my hands on such information concerning naxalite activities in the states in India which are now affected, extending from Andhra Pradesh to Nepal.

A great service that a Forum like this is discharging would be to painstakingly catalogue information and make it available for dissemination among the people so that they can undertake analysis and can draw their own conclusions. The second is that when something major occurs there should be a very comprehensive inquiry into all aspects of that issue. I have brought with me the report of the 9/11 Commission by the US Administration to go into the World Trade Towers attack. I don't know whether anyone of you has had the opportunity to see this. It is published in two volumes : one is the report and the other is some supporting documents. It's a splendid report. You know that it was a bipartisan commission which consisted of five representatives of the republican party and five of the democrats and it is a unanimous report. You know how politically sensitive the issue had been in those last few months, preceding the presidential election. Despite that they were able to produce a unanimous report without any dissenting notes. It is a splendid document because it doesn't waste too much space in setting at the voluminous evidence. The first chapter states the conclusions. It starts with each flight number, minute or second by second, puts down the chronology of events right in the first chapter. Then they have gone into the entire gamut of issues which made it possible for the designs of the terrorists to succeed which effected the responses. The report goes into issues like immigration, flight control, checking and the response systems. So you can see from the report that here is a nation which is of course seriously shaken by what happened but which has the will to build a very comprehensive framework of an action plan.

I do not know whether our way of setting up of inquiry commissions, which are more or less judicial forums which adjudicate on the basis of affidavits received from interested quarters, can generate this kind of report. We cannot afford to ignore the value of 9/11 type commissions. I am not suggesting that a young forum like yours undertake a major effort at inquiry but I think some thinking needs to be done as to how and when major events take place, how we can take advantage of those events and re-equip ourselves to deal with the challenges. We had the attack on Parliament. We were able to secure the conviction of the perpetrators within first one year from the occurrence and that was efficient and good work but after that the exercise ended. There was some committee in the Parliament Secretariat which went into assignments of security. They were beefed up here and there but that's not where the issue should have ended. I think a more comprehensive way to look at the matter is necessary so that such tragedies can be converted into opportunities for taking good initiatives.

I would like to make a point that, of late, there have been very disturbing signs of weakening of the will of the centre in dealing with the problem of insurgency. This weakening has taken place rather rapidly. Why it has happened and whether it is the compulsion of coalition. I don't know. That is a matter for discussion. But why do I say so! I would draw your attention to two specific developments which have taken place and that have given rise to this feeling in my mind. One is the whole episode of the repeal of POTA. You know that POTA was a time bound law; it was due to expire any way on the 24th October in year 2004 and then the question before the government would have been whether to extend the law or to re-enact it in a different form. The Government issued two ordinances on 21st September, that is just a month before the scheduled expiry of that law. By the first ordinance they repealed POTA. It was a frivolous act. Such are not actions which a serious Government takes. I can not put a meaning to this except in terms of appeasement of certain political groups.

In my other perspective it is difficult to explain why POTA had to be repealed on 21st September when it was in any case going to expire on the 24th October. In subsection 6 of section 1 of POTA even the action which has to be taken at the time of expiry in residual action is spelt out. There is nothing that this repealing ordinance has achieved except to give the impression that the Government has taken this action in subordination to its political convenience. Secondly, I don't think that POTA should have been repealed. What they have done is that on one hand they have repealed, POTA; on the other hand, all the penal provisions have been picked up and have been off-loaded to a pre-existing law called the unlawful, Activities Prevention Act, 1967. All the offences even the lists of terrorist organisations which existed in POTA have been annexed to the amended Unlawful Activities Prevention Act.

Surely the government must have thought that repeal of POTA is politically necessary; so let us do that but let us take the penal provisions into a milder sounding pre-existing law. I think this is not a serious action. But while doing so they have dropped all the special provisions concerning bail, confessions before police officer, the control of funds of terrorist organisations and interception of communications. These are vital for enforcement of the offences relating to terrorist acts. Just having the offences is meaningless, unless you have the instruments to enforce them. Those have been dropped and imagine what else has been dropped. There is a review committee under POTA, the advice of which is binding. The review committee consisted of a retired chief justice of the Punjab and Haryana High Court Justice Saharia and was undertaking review of all cases and had given relief in many cases and I think this was a good committee. It was a very good safeguard against the possible misuse of POTA. Now that committee has been dropped from 21st September 2005. There will be no committee to which there will be recourse. I do not know why it has been done and of course, there are other legal complications, which I need not elaborately raise before you.

The Government action of 21st September 2004 is an amalgam of feebleness, lack of will and mischief. When I say 'mischief', let me explain what I mean. Under the Un-lawful Activities Prevention Act, certain associations can be declared unlawful if they are. I remember when this law was enacted in late 60's, I used to be in the Home Ministry. Then it was seen as an assault on the right of association and there was a great debate in which people like Madhu Limay and Nath Pai and even communist leader Bhupesh Gupta had participated. There were pitched battles in Parliament because it was the first law in Independent India which was seen as an assault on the right of association.

After a vigorous debate, there was a consensus in the country that the law should apply only to organisations which worked for secession, that is challenging the integrity of India. That is how the Plebiscite Front was declared unlawful; the Mizo National Front was declared unlawful. Now what this Government has done is that it has introduced an addition to the definition of the unlawful association whereby any organisation which indulged in activities akin to section 153 AIPC can also be declared unlawful. Obviously it has been done to try and create an opening to assault the BJP related organisations. Unfortunately, the regional parties which are participating in the UPA have missed the point that the same provision can be used against them because many of them espouse regional causes. The mischief is that expanding the definition of unlawful association has been surreptitiously done. Such conduct of the Government does not reflect a mind which is serious and which treats the challenge of terrorism as the most serious challenge before the country.

The second point which I would like to bring to your notice is in relation to what the government has been doing about the challenge of naxalism. I believe that currently the greatest challenge to orderly society in this country is naxalism. Right from Andhra Pradesh to Nepal the entire corridor has been affected. According to the statement of the Union Home Minister, 125 districts in the country are effected by naxalite violence; other 25 are threatened, which makes it about 1/3rd of the country. Vast areas have been declared as "liberated" areas where the writ of the state police doesn't run. I am told that in the state of Jharkhand 21 out of 22 districts are affected. On the 21st of September, 2004 the very day on which all these naxalite organisations were also declared unlawful under the Unlawful Activities Prevention Act, there was a meeting of the Chief Ministers of the states affected by naxalite violence. The government of Andhra Pradesh had started its negotiations. But the other Chief Ministers objected to it saying, *inter alia* that the period of talks will be used by the naxalites to increase their strength, to gather more weapons because of the suspension of the operation by the security forces. The other states are not necessarily against talks but want the talks to be held by the Central Government so that each state doesn't go its own way.

The Chief Ministers' viewpoints were brushed aside and the Union Home Minister is reported to have told the chief ministers that you hold your talks. In fact he told the Chief Minister of AP that you hold your talks; if you succeed well and good if you don't succeed we won't blame you. These were the words which were reported in the press. He said that this is a public order issue and therefore it is within the responsibility of the States; if they want any support that support will be given by the Centre. This is the position Union Home Minister has taken. I think it is grossly faulty. I am saying this because the question arose as to in whose domain the acts of terrorism are. It arose in a case relating to Punjab, Kartar Singh's case in 1994. It was a five-judge bench of the Supreme Court which decided the case and the issue was the legality of TADA which was the predecessor law of POTA. Two aspects were examined. One was whether the centre had the legislative authority to enact TADA and the second related to the constitutionality of the various provisions; whether they violated the fundamental rights. I will not go into the second aspect. On the first aspect, the five judges gave a unanimous judgment that it was within the legislative domain of the centre. There are various entries in the seventh schedule which had to be examined and it had to be seen as to with which entry the pith and substance of TADA could be related. The first entry to be examined was entry *one* in the Union List, which is the defence of India. Then there is the residual entry 97, i.e. any matter which does not fall in any of the lists becomes a union subject under entry 97. Then entry 93 of the Union List concerning offences against laws with respect to any matter in the Union List. In the State list is entry 1, public order about which Mr. Shivraj Patil is supposed to have said that is the relevant entry when you are dealing with matters of terrorism. Then in the Concurrent list there is an entry relating to criminal law. All this was examined by the Supreme Court and the Court said the law and order is one thing, public order is another and acts of terrorism are quite another. The court referred to that famous observation made by Chief Justice Hidayatullah in 1964, that law and order, public order and security of the state may be viewed as three concentric circles. As far as the security of the state is concerned it is the innermost circle and is purely the responsibility of the centre.

The Supreme Court has now said clearly that it is not public order entry of the State list which encompasses terrorism. It is either the residual entry 97 or it is defence of India entry which covers terrorism. So they say it is within the exclusive domain of the centre to legislate in relation to terrorism. The consequences of this is that as the legislative and the executive authority coincide, to deal with terrorism is within the executive domain of the Center. That's the law of the land. How could the Union Home Minister say that dealing with terrorism is primarily the responsibility of the states. When it is a threat to the civilised society, when it is a threat to orderly government and is a threat to the security of the country? How can the Central Home Minister take that position that it is primarily the responsibility of the states. This thinking is fundamentally faulty. Does it only reflect escapism that you let the states take their initiatives in the matter and you stand behind and support! I don't think so. You can not indulge in such escapism. Dealing with terrorism is the responsibility of the centre and from this a lot of consequences follow. The question of funding arises. The financial responsibility has to be carried by the Centre. There is reason to believe that the passive approach chosen by the Central government is a payback for the electoral support given by the naxalites to the Congress Party in the recent elections in Andhra Pradesh. These two developments, that is the repeal of POTA, the manner in which political expediency and mischief has guided the way of dealing with naxalities show a lack of seriousness, and flaw in the thinking of the Centre in respect of its own responsibility.

Finally, I would like to refer to the position in the North-East. I have had the privilege o work in the North-East in two states. I was District Magistrate of Manipur when it used to be a single district in the mid-60's. As you know that Manipur has more Naga areas than Nagaland itself. Naga areas of Ukhrul, Tamenglong and Maroare are all in Manipur. When I was there, the cessation of operations agreement, which applied in Nagaland, did not apply to Manipur. So we had active insurgency in those days. I have a fair idea of the situation in Manipur and the way it has been mishandled in many subsequent years. I have worked as Chief Secretary in Arunachal Pradesh. We didn't have any district directly affected by insurgency except that the two districts of Tirap and Changlang, adjoining Nagaland, which were used as routes by the NSCN. So the problems had started in 1987-1988 when I was there. Now of course, the problem is more serious in the south bank districts of Arunachal Pradesh. I think what is being done in Northeast to ameliorate the socio-economic conditions which are the basis of insurgency is mere tokenism. I assume that you are familiar with the reorganisation of North-East and the position of the Northeast Council. Let me tell you that when this reorganisation took place in 1970 I used to be in the Ministry of Home Affairs. I was involved in the writing of the papers which led to the reorganisation. This reorganisation was undertaken when it was realised that continued dominance of Ahoms through the maintenance of greater Assam had not served the purpose of obviating threats to the integrity of the region. They were not able to play the kind of enlightened role which a dominant people in that region should have and they could not carry their tribal brethren along. So it was decided to let balkanisation take place in the Northeast and the seven states were created. The understanding at that time was that we would have a very strong North-Eastern Council and this North-Eastern Council had a role in development as well as a role in security. If you pay attention the North-Eastern Council Act, it is as strong on security as on development. That security rôle of the North-Eastern Council would be by way of a harmonised management in the North-Eastern region. But sheer negligence has burried the attetion to security role. The functioning of the North-Eastern Council needs serious attention to reinstale its security role, prudently written in the law alongside the development role. That is *one* point.

The *second* is that even in the field of development whatever has been done is not enough, nothing substantial is being done there and great opportunities for development are being ignored. The main stream of Brahmaputra consists of two rivers, one is called Siang or Dihang and the other is called Subansiri and there are the various tributary systems from the South and from the North. On Siang there is a site for a hydel project at a place called Pasighat, which can generate 20,000 megawatt of hydro electricity. It's the largest hydro site in the world after Amazon has been implemented by Brazil and Columbia. The pondage at Pasighat will result in the flood level in Guwhati coming down by a metre and a half, which means that the floods in the valley of Assam really disappear. The valley of Assam has something like 16 to 18 waves of flood in a single rainy season and all those can be obviated. The Siang project was one of the first projects, investigated by the World Bank in the early 50's and when I was in Arunachal Pradesh I had done some calculations and you will be surprised to know that at the 1987 prices, the generation cost of electricity came to 19 paise a unit and today it may be 50 or 60 paise that's about it. I still remember the population to be displaced was just 3,500 in a project which was going to generate 20,000 megawatts of electricity. Similarly, on the other stream that is Subansiri, there is a place along where there is a site which can generate 8,000 megawatts of electricity. Nothing has been done on these projects. What has been done is ordering of feasibility studies. When you cannot take decision, order a feasibility study; that is the approach of convenience adopted all these years. Similarly, in the matter of transportation there was a proposal which the NDA government had more or less approved to extend the golden quadrilateral project to cover the Assam highway both on the north bank as well as the south bank. It will provide employment on a massive scale. Along the highway, a new focus of development will emerge. The total annual budget of the North-Eastern Council which is supposed to undertake all the regional projects in these seven states may not be more than Rs. 300-400 crores a year. We are indulging in tokenism. But nothing has been done for the North-East in terms of substantial development.

4

The Threat of Left Wing Extremism: CPI(M)

Arun Bhagat

"No word ever dies. What we are saying today may not be accepted by the people at this moment. But our propaganda is not in vain. Our words remain embedded among the people." So said Charu Mazumdar during the Naxalbari movement.

Starting in May 1967 this movement petered out by 1972. However similar movements sprang up in other parts of the country in Srikakulam, Debra Gopiballavpur, Birbhum, and Bhojpur. Now communist extremists subscribing to different interpretations and lines within Marxism, Leninism, Maoism and Naxalism have their presence in 5 of the 7 South Asian countries. The only exceptions are Pakistan and Maldives where there are no groups as yet. In India there are more than 35 groups. Continuous separations, divisions and sub-divisions have marked the Communist movement in India. So has it been with those who broke away from the communist mainstream to take up arms and not votes as a means to acquire power.

The two main Naxal groups, the CP (ML) Peoples War and the MCC merged in 2004 to form the CPI (Maoist). The two groups were responsible for 80 to 85% of all left wing violence in the country in any given year. As many as 13 States are directly affected by left wing extremism. The CPI (M) claim they have their presence in 15 states. A Government expert estimates that over 22 crore citizens residing in over 120 districts are affected by this form of extremism. Prior to the peace talks held in August, 2004, with the Government of Andhra Pradesh, the Secretary of the Peoples War, Ramakrishna alias Hargopal said that their ultimate goal was to liberate the people from the evils of capitalist forces and that they had come to participate in the talks on equal terms. Further that they did not believe that the suffering masses could be liberated through negotiations. There will be no compromise on their ideology, he said and there was no question of giving up armed struggle irrespective of the outcome of the talks. He admitted that peace talks formed a part of political strategy. His choice of words is significant. The Peoples War Group considers itself to be on an equal footing with the legally established Government. That the AP government went ahead with the talks, after this plain speak by the extremists, indicates that the seriousness of the situation and the dangers they pose in the future is not realised.

In this paper I propose to examine the development and growth of the ideologies, which guide and steer radical left wing extremism and its contemporary and future impact on the country.

The roots of Left wing extremism in the country can be traced to agrarian movements, which go as far back as the 18th century. The Congress party itself made land reforms, land to the tiller, abolition of Zamindari and a host of other socio-economic issues a part of their objectives. Prior to independence these genuine issues won them the mass support to achieve the larger goal of freedom from the colonial rulers. Most of the agrarian movements were however spontaneous. Organised agitations were to come later. The Champaran Satyagraha also referred to as the Indigo Peasants Movement of 1917 in which Gandhiji himself participated, was possibly the first. In 1930, Bihar Provincial Kisan Sabha (BPKS) led by Swami Sahajanand was formed, which focused on the grievances of tenants against Bhumihar landlords. Contemporaneously, the Triveni Sangh was formed as a socio-political organisation of the backward classes in Bihar.

The Tehbaga movement in Bengal (1946-47) sought to reduce the 50% share of crops to landlords to 1/3rd. Indian communists had earlier formed the Worker's and Peasants Party in 1926 in Bengal. Other groups were active in the province like the *Bengal Kisan Sabha,* a local wing of the *All India Kisan Sabha* established in 1936. Another significant movement was in Telengana between 1946 and 1951. This struggle became enmeshed with the struggle against the Nizam when he refused to merge with independent India. The Communists played a leading part and formed armed squads called *dalams,* a term which continues till now. Four thousands villages were brought under *gram rajyams* or parallel government. Even after the Police action in Hyderabad, the communist movement continued and faced severe action from the authorities. It was only in October 1951 that the Communist Party decided to withdraw the armed peasant struggle.

Post-independence, all states passed legislation to try to implement their promises to the people and remove the more glaring and multiple forms of inequities and exploitation, which the peasantry had to suffer. The legislative measures varied from state to state. The peasants and the landless were subjected to different forms of exploitation which in some areas had virtually become traditionally accepted practices. Bonded labour was common. Similarly, the tenants were required to work free on many occasions during the year. Sexual exploitation was also prevalent. These could not be redressed by legislation alone particularly when the Congress party, which virtually ruled over the whole country continuously for the first 3 decades, drew its strength from the rich farmers and traders in the countryside. They remained the direction-givers and vote-garnerers for the Party.

In many states the benefits of the land distribution legislation could never reach the tenants. The rural landless labour and the tribals were the other major groups, in most states, whose lot worsened after independence. The agrarian movement post independence has been closely linked with efforts of the backward castes to gain their rightful place in society. This brief historic background clearly shows that the agrarian problem has been endemic in the country and failure to find correct and effective solutions has led to the creation of a situation in the country which spawns discontent and provides support to left wing groups. They are not incorrect when they say that poverty and exploitation has not been removed. We perforce also have to agree with them that many citizens do not enjoy the fundamental rights enshrined in the Constitution. However, the extremists hark back to a failed and discarded ideology which clearly is not the solution.

Naxalbari movement has been well documented and researched. I will, therefore, restrict myself to a critique of the movement as analysed by communists themselves, scholars and experts. Charu Mazumdar hoped to create a countrywide upsurge and all along maintained that the rising was imminent and was coming. He adopted the strategy of establishing multiple bases and hoped that these would rapidly increase in numbers and join with each other to cover larger and larger areas. Accretion to the limited strength of the cadres, he thought, would follow the spontaneous upsurge and positive response of the masses to the Naxalite policy of annihilation. Mazumdar favoured the use of implements of common use like knives, axes and sickles to arms and ammunition. Many senior leaders of the group expressed their reservations about the strategy. The pro-Charu group was however, very powerful and stiffled all criticism. They projected Charu as the supreme leader arguing that the movement could only succeed if there was a single revolutionary authority. Charu's statement that China's Chairman was our Chairman did not find many takers. In fact the memories of the Chinese attack were still fresh and his declaration was resented by the general public. No attempt was made to set up village level committees.

In one of their assessments of the movement in March, 1971, the Andhra State Committee of the CPI (ML) observed, "Our cadres are predominantly petit bourgeois. Even today the villages of poor and landless peasants are not the centres of our activity. .... This is our fundamental weakness." The West Bengal-Bihar Border Committee in September 1971 noted 'we ignored political and ideological work in respect of peasant guerillas ... we could not develop a greater number of organisers and political commissars from among poor and landless peasants cadres and guerillas'. Annihilation of class enemies was the only goal set forth. This, Mazumdar thought, would spark off the prairie fire as Mao had held out. Furthermore, there was no hinterland where when pressed, the cadres could retreat. Neither was any external assistance forthcoming. The Chinese Communist Party conveyed its disapproval of Mazumdar's statement about Mao and noted that it would wound national sentiments. They also conveyed that the theory of annihilation needed to be reviewed. That the People's War Theory of Lin Piao could not be applied in a mechanical manner. To sustain the movement, mass struggle and mass organisation was necessary. The movement lacked organisational structures as well.

The announcement of the Peoples War (PW) and the Maoist Communist Centre of India (MCCI) merging to form the CPI(M) was made just before the peace talks between the Government of Andhra Pradesh and the PWG began. The timing of the announcement is significant. Of the over 30 odd left extremist groups in the country these two were by far the strongest. After the All India Coordination Committee of Communist Revolutionaries split in May 1969 and the CPI (ML) was formed, a small group led by Amulya Sen and Kanai Chatterjee decided to keep away from the new party. A few months later they formed their own group and named it Dakshin Desh. Sometime later, they took on a new name and called themselves the Maoist Communist Centre. This name continued till their merger about 2 years back with a much smaller group of Naxalites going by the name of the Revolutionary Communist Center of India (Maoist). After the merger the MCC renamed itself MCCI. Another group bearing the name the Second Central Committee of the CPI (ML) merged with the MCCI. Strongly advocating the purist ideological line they constantly oppose the 'revisionists' who they allege seek to dilute and stray from the path of armed struggle.

The MCCI perception of Indian society is that it is semi-feudal and semi-colonial; further that it suffers from two contradictions. Firstly, peasantry versus feudal elements; secondly, imperialism against the peasantry, workers and the oppressed bourgeoisie. They believe that these contradictions would come to a head and lead to 1) a democratic revolution and 2) an eruption of a national revolution, which in turn would eliminate the imperial class. To achieve the first objective, a mass base among the people particularly the peasantry had to be built. Deep politicisation of the masses was a pre-condition. Propaganda cum education teams should be given responsibility for this. As class enemies like landlords, moneylenders and other reactionaries would oppose them armed squads should be formed of committed cadres. The squads would deal with selected class enemies and guard the peasants and workers from exploitation. They would be instrumental in the establishment of red bases & red safe areas. The next step would be the formation of a people's army. Political power can only be seized through armed struggle, they believe.

The MCC plan was to be implemented in three stages. The *first* stage envisaged the use of propaganda to organise mass resistance movements against oppression by moneylenders, landlords, and demand equal treatment in social, political and economic spheres. The MCC perceives this would raise the level of political consciousness of the masses and prepare them to challenge the existing system. The *second* stage involves revolutionary peasants adopting the line of annihilation of class enemies and defending themselves against reprisals. Reprisals would be answered by counter attacks on the powerful classes and their agents, meaning the government. Arms would be snatched and defensive struggle launched against state forces. The third stage would bring the revolutionary masses in direct conflict with the reactionary armed forces. The MCC has been using handbills, posters, *dharnas*, public meetings, nukkad discussions, protests and demonstrations effectively. Landlords and other class enemies are issued threats, told to pay fines and penalties. Physical attacks and assassinations are also common. Social and economic blockades are organised.

A large number of front organisations sponsored by the MCCI work openly for them. Among them are *Jan Suraksha Sangharsh Manch, Krantikari Budhijivi Sangh, Krantikari Sanskriti Manch.* While they say they resort only to selective, targeted violence against class enemies, they have been responsible for wanton mass killings of civilians including women and children. The MCCI have set up *Krantikari Kisan Committees* (KKC) in villages. KKC's have as their slogan 'izzat and azadi 'and take up multifarious local issues. The KKC look into individual complaints and hold jan adalats, which pass judgments, impose penalties and fines. Collection of 'taxes' is another responsibility given to the KKC. To maintain discipline, cadres are subjected to severe punishments and are required to pay $1/7^{th}$ of their annual income. Seizure and distribution of land, conduct of local works, gathering intelligence are other tasks assigned to the KKC. A portion of the land seized is earmarked to grow seeds by the KKC and the rest is given for cultivation to the landless. They also run schools and provide free rudimentary health care.

Recruitment, identification of class enemies, intelligence gathering, garnering support for demonstrations, selection of hideouts are among the other tasks assigned to the KKC. The strongholds of the MCC are largely in Bihar and Jharkhand. They have a presence in Sundargarh and Keonjhar districts of Orissa. They are expanding their activities in Burdwan, Nadia, Howrah and 24 Parganas districts in West Bengal. Mirzapur, Chandauli and Sonbhadra in UP are other areas where they have made significant inroads. They have constituted what they call *Peoples Liberation Guerilla Army.*

Kodapali Seetharamiah, a member of the Central Organising Committee of the CPI (ML) played a major role in setting up Peoples War Group as it is generally known. The 22nd of April, the date of birth of Lenin, was chosen in 1980 to announce its formation. Its lesser known but formal name was CPI (ML)(PW). A firm protagonist of the Naxalite path and fervent adherent of Mao, he set up base in Karimnagar district of north Telengana. The group believed in Mao's theory of peasant rebellions and rejects the Constitution of India. Like Mao they believe that political power can be achieved only through the barrel of the gun and their goal is to establish a people's government to bring about a *New Democratic Revolution.* The Group organised armed squads called *Dalams* and soon had as many as 50 active in Telengana. Over the years they have gained considerable strength. Their spread and growth has been helped by the absence of a consistent policy on the part of the Government not only in Andhra but also in the other states where they have made significant inroads. Over the past 13 years, the PWG has been responsible for the destruction of property worth thousand of crores in Andhra alone. Public and private property has been targeted since the group started operating.

The Central Committee (CC) with 21 members was at the head of the organisational structure of the erstwhile PWG. Muppala Lakshmana Rao @ Ganapati was the General Secretary. Other members were C.Rajkumkar @ Davanna @ Uday @ Madhu, M.Koteswara Rao and N. Keshava Rao @ Ganganna. Naveen Prasad, Sumit and Surjit of the Party Unity Group which merged with the PWG finds a place in the CC. The secretaries of state committees of Bihar, West Bengal, Karnataka, Maharashtra and members of the Military Commission also served on the CC. Under the CC were Regional Bureaus, also known as Zonal or State Committees, Division or District Committees, squad area committees and the village governance committees. The armed wing was under the Central Military Commission (CMC) which was headed by the General Secretary of the CC. Parallel military committees had been formed corresponding to each level of the political structure. The PWG formed the *People's Guerilla Army* (PGA) in December 2000 with its own insignia and flag. Organised as platoons consisting of 40 persons they rely on mobility, knowledge of the terrain, field craft, surprise, meticulous planning based on intelligence and surveillance. Accurate information of their strength is not forthcoming, but given their presence in 10 to 12 states, they should have about 100 platoons.

In addition there would be much larger numbers bearing arms in the *dalams* or the village level armed squads. These are sometimes referred to as the local or the central guerilla squads.

They developed what they call the People's militia in some areas. The organisation they set up is layered modeled on the pattern of a government hierarchy. While believing in strict central control a number of special zones were formed. The North Telengana, Andhra-Orissa Border, Dandakarayana Spl. Zones and the Andhra Pradesh State Committee enjoyed considerable autonomy. Separate Guerilla Zones were constituted for North and South Telengana and northern coastal region of Andhra. A number of what they call *Permanent Action Teams* comprising 3 to 4 members were formed which were special exclusive cells entrusted with assassination of specific persons. The task was given to the leader of the cell who alone was in touch with the higher leadership. Members of the cell are known to the leader alone and come together only to carry out the task or to rehearse the same. Highly motivated and well trained in the use of weapons and related tradecraft they have been known to prepare for months before carrying out their assignment. Their success rate is reported to be very high.

The PWG has been very resilient and have changed their strategy from time to time. They firmly believe that protracted people's war is the only path to seize political power and that the parliamentary path is not the solution for the oppressed masses and nationalities of the country. This they hope to achieve through 1) The Party 2) the Army and 3) the United Front. Consolidation of their hold on liberated areas is foremost in their strategy. "Don't leave the enemy forces unhurt, once it enters our area" is a slogan they stress. Secondly expand into new areas. Thirdly weaken civil authority and create conditions, which compel the people to lose their faith and trust in the established order. The PWG local level committees backed by the armed wing then step in to offer solutions. They perceive that once their base support is enlarged, propaganda and terror would ensure that secure red bases are created which would cover ever-increasing areas till the whole country is engulfed. Assassinations, abductions, destruction of government property, kangaroo courts, attacks on police and security forces are the means they employ. Fear, terror, revenge and retaliation feature high in their strategy. Thus the attempt on the life of Chandra Babu Naidu.

Scores of over ground organizations have been created to work in tandem. Allegations of human rights violations, complaints, criminal and civil cases against individual officers, dharnas, demonstrations, protests to muddy the waters and divert attention from their own gory record of violence and destruction of public property are used effectively. While they do not believe in democracy they make full use of the liberties and the freedoms, which democratic India offers to weaken and suborn the state and make it non-functional. Another major plank is the promise of the right of all nationalities in India to independence. They support the terrorists in Jammu & Kashmir, the ULFA and even radical Islamist groups. This they assess will lead to the increase in turmoil and turbulence bringing in disorder, chaos allowing them to step in.

The new name adopted by the PWG and the MCCI following their merger is very significant. The merged group has dropped Marxist, Leninist from the new name of the party altogether. This however does not mean that the CPI (Maoist) has discarded Leninist-Marxist ideology. Far from it. Maoist communist ideologues hail Marxism as a science in which constant development is a natural process. New experiences and problems of class struggle had led Lenin to raise Marxism to the second stage of development, which they refer to as Leninism. Maoism represents the third, the new and higher stage of development. M-L-M is a total and integral entity of universal truth and Mao's thought, the Marxism-Leninism of the present day world, they contend. Mao, according to their interpretation established the law of contradiction as the essence of dialectical materialism. The fundamental law of dialectics pervades all fields of nature, society and human knowledge. Mao identified class struggle, struggle for production and scientific experiment as the source of all knowledge.

The ideologues hail the principles of political economy laid down by Mao in the socialist stage, which tried to increase the initiative of the masses in taking over production. At the same time they point out the measures taken under Mao in China to destroy feudalism, monopolies both foreign and local, control of private capital as necessary. To achieve the New Democratic Revolution they espouse People's War. In fact some even refer to the Great Proletarian Cultural Revolution in China as the third great communist revolution. A quote from Mao 'in the coming years the world will pass through great upheavals' is a favorite when referring to revisionist communists of China, the CPI or the CP (M). Maoist theorists see the people's war developing in three phases. The first is strategic defence when armed squads are organised, arms acquired, peoples militia formed, class enemies attacked, support of the masses for the ideology, gained and base areas created and defended. The second phase is referred to as strategic equilibrium when the Party establishes a People's army and gains near parity with the state forces. The third described as the qualitatively higher stage involves strategic offence when the people's army goes on the offensive for the final putsch to terminate the established or old order and seize political power.

The PWG and MCCI have developed close ties with the CPN (M) over the past few years. Along with the MCCI, prior to their merger and the Communist Party of Nepal (Maoist) the Coordination Committee of Maoist Parties and Organisation of South Asia (CCOMPOSA) was set up in July, 2001. Apart from the groups mentioned above Maoist groups from Sri Lanka and Bangladesh also participated in the deliberations and decided to coordinate their activities. After this meeting the Indo-Nepal Border Regional Committee was formed with the PWG, MCCI and CPN (M) as members to coordinate the pursuit of the revolutionary movement in India and Nepal. MCCI activities in the districts of Bihar and UP bordering Nepal increased considerably thereafter. Joint training camps were organised in Hazaribagh and Aurangabad. The CPN(M) perceived India as a semi-colonial, semi-feudal power with imperialist expansionist designs. They blame unequal treaties beginning with the Sugali Treaty of 1815 to be as responsible for Nepal's impoverishment as the feudal set up and the monarchy. A party document goes to the extent of saying that to achieve final victory the People's Army must prepare itself to take on the Indian army. The CPN (M) has seriously deliberated the declaration of an independent government in Nepal. Buoyed by their successes the leaders of the CPN (M) saw themselves as leading the revolution not only in the sub-continent but the whole world.

The Prachanda Path, formulated by the CPI (N) was the guide for the Nepal Maoists has been widely discussed and debated within the CPI (M) and articles by Nepal Maoists appear regularly in party publications. *Sendoro Luminoso* or the Shining Path of the Peruvian left wing extremists has influenced the radical communist ideology of the Nepalese Maoists. They also draw inspiration from the Revolutionary International Movement (RIM). Without formally adopting it, the Indian Maoists increasingly rely on it. The top leadership of Nepalese Maoists is well educated and have been prolific in their writings, which cover a wide range of subjects. They attach high importance to ideology and quote Mao as saying 'Correctness and incorrectness of ideological and political line decides everything. If the political line is correct everything will come in its way, if it is wrong everything will be lost'.

The leadership of the 11 year long Maoist insurgency in Nepal reviewed their strategy as they found that a stalemate had been reached and their earlier successes had failed to generate the spontaneous uprising they had hoped for. Their cadres had started deserting. Over 7½ lakhs had left their homes in the conflict zones and the areas controlled by the Maoists and migrated to other parts of Nepal and India. The peasantry as well as the urban dwellers were aghast at the bloodbath which has taken over 10,000 lives. Pro-democracy political parties raised the level of civil protests against the Monarch who had dissolved the elected Parliament and taken over the reins of the government. The CPI (M) leaders Prachanda & Bhatrai decided to join the Nepali Congress and 6 other parties in the civil disobedience movement. In the face of a united opposition, civil unrest and pressure from some foreign countries King Gyanendra was compelled to appoint G.P. Koirala of the Nepali Congress as the Prime Minister in April, 2006. The Maoists immediately announced a 3 month ceasefire. Following protracted secret negoations between the 7 party alliance and the Maoists in Delhi, the Maoist have agreed to accept Parliamentary democracy and participate peacefully in the elections of an assembly to form a new constitution for the country and subsequent elections to the Parliament. Many contentious issues persist like the surrender of arms, the rehabilitation of the armed cadres, return of private property seized by the Maoists and a host of other issues but the leaders have shown a rare sense of history, pragmatism and statesmanship in accommodating each other views and appear to be working together to chart a new chapter to establish democracy in the country. The fate of the Monarchy is in fine balance as Gyanendra with his actions has gnawed away at his own support base. The spectra of the sad end of King Mahendra and his whole family, still remains shrouded in mystery and casts a dark shadow on the monarchy.

The PW and the MCCCI have well trained and tested cadres who have gained expertise in the use of IED's, laying ambushes and carrying out attacks on police station and patrols. They not only plan the attacks very carefully but also conduct critical analysis of both their successes and failures. That they have developed capability to conduct large-scale attacks was shown by their success when they took over the Koraput district headquarters in Orissa. On the night of February 6th 2004 over 200 armed guerillas of the PW carried out simultaneous attacks on the Police Lines, the District jail, the office of the SP, the rural and town police stations and the district Treasury in Koraput. A unit of the Orissa Special Armed Police located near the town, which could have sent reinforcements was attacked at the same time to keep them engaged. This proved to be a successful diversion. The single sentry on duty at the Police Lines armory was shot dead. Party publications claim they looted over 500 weapons including LMG's, mortars, grenades, SLR's and .303 rifles. About 30,000 rounds of ammunition were carried away. They took about 2 dozen other weapons from the Jail, SP's office and the Treasury. Loud speakers were used to warn the people not to come out and the police to surrender.

The surprise element was such that there was virtually no resistance. The attacks were swift and the different groups of guerillas appeared to have fully rehearsed their tasks. Government vehicles were used to carry the attackers and their booty to different points in the jungles. A large number of police vehicles were burnt to disable their use in hot pursuit. While retreating they attacked three more police stations and a Dy. SP's office. Land mines were planted on three main roads leading to the town on the routes reinforcements were likely to take and ambush parties placed. A CRPF relief party rushing to Koraput became a prey in one ambush and lost three men. Half a dozen were injured. The PWG hailed it as a major success of their ongoing programme of 'Tactical counter-offensive campaign' to arm the People's Guerilla Army and compared it to the 1930 raid carried out in a similar manner by Indian revolutionaries in Chittagong. The PWG claim that units from the eight guerilla zones were brought in for the attack and they suffered no casualties as the policemen meekly surrendered. This and subsequent attacks clearly show the seriousness of the threat faced by the country and the capabilities which the CPI (M) has developed.

The organisational structure of the CP (M) is not fully known. The highest policy making body is the Central Committee which has been enlarged to accommodate all the constituents. The other bodies are the Politburo, the Military Commission and State and Regional Commissions. The MCCI had its main strength and strongholds in Bihar, Jharkhand and Orissa while the PWG concentration was in Andhra, Orissa, Chattisgarh, Karnataka and Maharashtra. There was an overlap in Bihar, Orissa, West Bengal and Jharkhand. Satisfying the local leadership of the two groups could face obstacles. For the past about three years, there has been regular interaction between the leaders and some joint actions at local levels as well. However, sharing of finances and arms could be tricky. Both outfits have sizable funds collected through what they call money actions and other means. Bank robberies, ransom from abductions, extortions from contractors, transporters, business, industry and individuals including government and private sector employees, fines and penalties have been their source of income. According to one estimate, the MCCI collects over Rs. 200 crores every year. Each group has very large holdings of arms and ammunition. Organisational and disciplinary problems can be anticipated.

The threat which the merger now poses is real and can no longer be ignored or wished away. We all know what is required to be done. Post independence, we are no strangers to rebellions, extremism, terrorism, brigandage, riots and the like. Nearly every state in the country has faced these problems at some time or the other. The expertise and experience as well as the wherewithal is there in the country. But we have a weakness of allowing matters to drift till the problem aggravates and gains menacing proportions. Certainly left wing extremism is a multi-dimensional problem involving multiple issues of development, education, unemployment, economic progress, education and ineffectual public services. Yet at the core is our inability to look at it holistically. The Maoists talk about a United Front. We also need a united front and uniformity in facing the menace. The time for flip flop, on and off is over. The Maoists cannot be allowed to utilise the boundaries of states to slip away. That is why their concentration is on borders. Bihar, Jharkhand, Jharkhand Orissa, Andhra and so on. A long-term view and a perspective has to be taken and a consistent policy adopted which should be sustained, irrespective of elections and the complexion of those at the helm in the states and the centre. Coordination between the states has to be improved in areas of both intelligence generation and sharing. Real time exchange of information and joint action groups to carry out hot pursuit and operations have to be rehearsed and perfected. Like the guerillas strategy the weakest areas if tackled foremost, cleared and secured, will lead to shrinkage of affected territory and their speedy elimination. The reality of the failed doctrine of radical communism and the dictatorship of the proletariat, which is a euphemism for totalitarianism, has to be brought home through effective publicity. That the slogans and promises are mere rhetoric and have no basis in reality as seen from the experiences of erstwhile USSR, East Germany, Poland, Romania, Cambodia, Vietnam and a host of other countries is recent history. They were all totalitarian regimes under whom, the people suffered. It is a recorded fact that well entrenched but enlightened leaders of the Communist parties themselves realised that Marxism-Leninism could not be the vehicle for prosperity for the people and they themselves were instrumental in dismantling the all-pervasive Party. At the same time, our delivery systems whether it is basic amenities like drinking water, electricity, education have to reach every citizen of the country. The Rule of Law enshrined in our Constitution has to be ensured to each and every citizen of the country wherever located. Unfortunately it still remains a distant dream. The burden rests on all of us but more so on the political leadership who have still to learn that India is larger and the citizens more important than mere victories in elections. Compromises and reluctance to squarely face problems is as much a danger to the security and integrity of India as left wing terrorism.

5

National Security — The Internal Dimension

General (Retd.) V P Malik

National Security implies *'the ability of a nation to use its national power for the preservation, protection that means integrity, and furtherance of its core values or national aims and objectives '.*

Kautilya said that the 'worst enemy is the enemy within'. In *Arthashastra,* he stated, "Arrows may not kill a soldier but skillful intrigue can kill even those in the womb." From *Kautiliya's Arthshastra* and national security viewpoint, internal and external security is meshed. After 9/11, this meshing has been acknowledged by the world more than ever before. Let me explain this with our own example and I will start from outside.

Currently, the whole of South Asia— India, Nepal, Bangladesh, Sri Lanka, Maldives, and Pakistan— is going through internal unrest and upheavals due to insurgency movements, ethnic conflicts, religious fundamentalism, or just cussed political polarisation. Such unrests have a history of crossing national boundaries and leading to inter-state tensions.

Geo-politically, South Asia represents an integral security zone with India's unique centrality. No two South Asian nations can interact with each other directly without touching or crossing

Indian land, sea or air space. India has special ties with each of her neighbours— of ethnicity, language, culture, common historical experience, or of shared access to vital natural resources like water— of a degree of intensity that is not shared by any two others. We do not have serious territorial security problem with neighbours other than China and Pakistan. But there are issues like the Indian secessionist groups using neighbours' territory as sanctuaries, trans border illegal migration, gunrunning and narcotics. The neighbourly unrests, therefore, have special significance and security implications for India.

Let us now look within India! India has a huge diversity— one billion spread over approximately 3.1 million square kilometers of territory. We speak 16 major languages and over 200 dialects. We have about one dozen ethnic groups, 7 major religion communities with several sects and sub-sects, and 68 socio-cultural sub-regions. When a socio-political and socio-economic equilibrium is maintained, there is unity in diversity. But a slight imbalance, and you have more diversity and less unity. This has been the hallmark of our history.... invariably exploited by outsiders.

Within India, even after 57 years of independence, our secular, open and pluralistic society continues to be vulnerable to several internal contradictions. Some specific issues that we are faced with are: —

- Problems of national assimilation and integration particularly of Border States in the North-East.
- Porous borders with Nepal, Bhutan, Myanmar, Bangladesh, and Sri Lanka which enable illegal trans border movements and smuggling of weapons and drugs. These days AK rifles, machine guns, rocket propelled grenades, land mines, RDX, even shoulder fired surface to air missiles are easily available in our neighbourhood. There is no way that we can guard or police every meter of these land, sea and air borders.
- Weak governance including law and order machinery and large-scale corruption. Nexus between crime, insurgency and politics.

Given our poverty, illiteracy, communal and casteist vote bank politics, these contradictions are unlikely to disappear soon. The internal security prognosis, therefore, should be a cause of serious concern for those in the national security apparatus. It is also apparent that our existing internal security policies and primary instruments for tackling law and order and internal security have not been able to cope up adequately with these growing challenges. In most troubled states, we have had to deploy large numbers of CPOs, PMF and the Army (including Rashtriya Rifles) to create a semblance of law and order, and create conditions wherein elections can be held for elected representatives to govern the state. Once committed, with few exceptions, these forces have remained there for decades.

Three points need to be made here.

First. Military pressure alone cannot resolve matters unless there is good governance and a strong thrust on socio-political and socio-economic issues. Political leadership and civil administration have to govern the states and the country with greater commitment and efficiency.

Second. Protracted employment of Army leads to "*Law of Diminishing Returns*". The reasons are (a) over dependence on the Army reflects lack of trust and faith in the capability of the state and central armed police and para military forces (b) after a while, locals treat the Army as another police force (c) such duties have adverse impact on Army's operational effectiveness (d) during a war/war like situation; Army needs public support. It cannot afford to alienate local population as is currently happening in Manipur and to some extent in J&K and Assam.

Third. Reduction in Army deployment will be possible only if we can revamp the para military, central and state police forces. We need to urgently modernise these forces, improve their leadership, training and man management. All this does not mean that the Army can stay away from internal security duties. That is Army's secondary responsibility.

Let me now come to some other specific problems and suggestions.

Law and order is a state subject. But the states have neither the money nor inclination to upgrade the quality of the state police or to raise any extra forces without substantial financial help from the Centre. They let the situation deteriorate. When it is too late, they seek assistance from the Centre. This responsibility without resources at the state level, and lack of accountability at state and Centre levels needs to be resolved. We must revise norms so that money for maintenance of law and order machinery is adequate. It is not diverted or pocketed. We must take steps to reduce political interference in the duties of IPS offices. I will not go into details of this aspect but feel that it is for the IPS officers to come out with such a demand and suggestions.

When a particular serious law and order spreads in a region, like the North-East or Naxalites and PWG in the central belt of India, the states must accept a coordinating role by the Centre. The Centre must establish an effective coordination of intelligence and operations through a regional set up. I have described how the external and internal security is meshed. How can Army operate effectively with state and central armed police forces and para military forces? A time has come to think in terms of integrated capabilities and synergy among the forces for optimum utilisation of military power. Synergy can be ensured only when our aims, goals, resources & techniques are harmonised by a single internal security doctrine. Greater liaison, coordination and inter operability for operations is needed with agencies responsible for internal security than we had so far. For the Army, that means Rashtriya Rifles. There must be adequate inter operability. The backbone of such interoperability is sets of common inter operable communication system and operating procedures.

Sometime ago the Army had proposed that for revamping state armed police, central police forces and para military forces, trained Army personnel with 8-10 years service be laterally inducted into these forces. They will not only bring in some Army ethos and culture but also save state money on training. The laterally inducted men will benefit by serving longer (more saving due to late receipt of pension) and within their own state. The Army will also benefit. It will be able to maintain a younger age profile. It will be a win-win situation for all.

We had also proposed that all young officers joining these forces be either trained in Army training establishments like the Indian Military Academy and Officers Training Academy, or their own commissioning establishments have instructors from the Army. Some Army officers in the ranks equivalent of Lieutenant Colonels and Colonels could also be selected for lateral induction into these forces. Most political leaders in the Government had favored this proposal. But it has not been implemented due to vested interests. It is time that we rose above our parochial interests.

Some suggestions that may be considered for improvement of policing and intelligence in Border States are as follows:

> Assam Rifles, had been raised primarily for deployment in the North-East and comprised personnel from these areas. Some years ago, its composition was changed to an all India composition force. The force thus lost its excellent rapport with local people, so essential for intelligence gathering and maintaining law and order. I feel that about 65-70 per cent of this force should be recruited from the North-East. With this composition, the battalions should be rotated within North-East on 3-4 years tenure basis and not allowed to develop 'material' interests in the local set up.

Considering the length of our borders, our border-holding forces will always remain inadequate. They have to be supplemented with 'home and hearth' units or village guards; of the kind that we had in Arunachal Pradesh. These 'home and hearth' units, with as many local ex-servicemen as possible, should be raised/deployed wherever border-holding forces are thin on the ground. They must maintain good communication and liaison with the latter. Army personnel should train these personnel on the lines of Border Scouts. Amongst the North-Eastern states, which are more vulnerable to internal and external security pressures, we also need more effective coordination of intelligence and operations through a regional set-up in Guwahati or Shillong. This can be established as a part of the North-East Council. A similar set up would need to be established in central India to counter Naxalite/Maoist threat.

The Armed Forces Special Powers Act has been much in the news for sometime. The situation is an after effect of prolonged employment of the Armed Forces in an area. Let me explain this and other instrument for employment of Armed Forces in internal security. We have two laws: CRPC Sections: 129-132 for calling Army to deal with unlawful assemblies, rioting, looting etc. situations—a lower level law and order situation. A collector can make use of this. One of these sections provides legal cover to the Armed Forces personnel. The other is AFSPA; for more serious situations like insurgencies, militancy, and widespread terrorism. The AFSPA (enacted by the Parliament in 1958) is currently the legal authority for troops to operate in insurgency and terrorism affected areas of J&K and North-East. Para 3 of the Act defines power to declare areas to be disturbed areas. It states that for using armed forces in aid of civil power, the Governor of that State/Union Territory or the Central Government has to, by Official Gazette Notification, declare the whole or affected part of the State to be a 'disturbed area'. Para 4 states that 'a commissioned officer, warrant officer, non commissioned officer or any other person of equivalent rank in the armed forces in a disturbed area, may:-

- Fire upon/use force, even to causing death, against any person contravening law and order or carrying weapons, ammunition or explosives, if in his opinion it is necessary for maintenance of law and order and after giving due warning. (The 'opinion' usually has to be justified subsequently.)
- Destroy armed dump or fortified position or shelter from which armed attacks can be made or can be used for training by hostiles, if necessary to do so.
- Arrest without warrant any person who has committed a cognisable offence and may use suitable force, if necessary to do so.

- Enter any premise without a warrant to arrest a terrorist/ suspect, or to recover a wrongfully confined person, stolen property, or arms/explosives wrongfully kept.

Para 5 of the Act lays down that the arrested persons will be handed over to the nearest police station with least possible delay alongwith the circumstances of the report.

In the current *impasse*, it is understandable that we do not wish to alienate people any more. The Govt. has ordered a review of AFSPA by a Justice J Reddy and his team within the next six months. What we have to ensure is to give a legal cover to our soldiers for the kind of operational duties that we expect him to perform.

Finally, we must have a comprehensive strategy to deal with insurgency and terrorism in Border States. That should include broad based domains of national and states' policies including accelerated economic development and elements of security and media policies. Most importantly, it should address dedicated and effective governance through good administration, prompt and fair judiciary and law and order machinery that inspire confidence. As has already been stated, *prevention is better than suffering and then seeking a cure.*

6

How Secured Are We From Within the Changing Paradigms of Security

Air Marshal (Retd.) Vinod Patney

"If you are out to describe the truth, leave elegance to the tailor."

— Albert Einstein

Introduction

The manner in which India has withstood the challenges facing a large underdeveloped country with a burgeoning population, is indeed creditable. Inevitably, there are any number of problems that confront us and, in our unique fashion, they are being addressed. However, a few major events over the last decade or so have altered the paradigms of security. The first development relates to the tremendous impact of scientific developments that, *inter alia*, include miniaturisation, phenomenal increase in computing power, and space applications. The manner of waging wars has markedly changed. Of particular interest is the availability of precision attack and long range weapon systems that have raised even a high probability of successful attacks to near certainty of success. The breakup of the erstwhile Soviet

Union resulted in a unipolar world with the USA often referred to as the hegemon. The changed political order facilitated the phenomenon of globalisation thereby increasing the interdependence of nations. Such interdependence has ensured that most nations have a stake in continued peace, as war almost anywhere will impact many other countries. This has lowered the probability of any major war.

In fact, the impact of the USA on the global scene is so overpowering, that it appears that a major war is highly unlikely unless the superpower is involved, or the war is fought in support of the superpower, or with the tacit approval of the superpower. Globalisation also increased competition and, for economic considerations, when business and industrial infrastructure is created, security aspects are often given reduced importance. As a result, 'many high value targets' are now more vulnerable to enemy action. The increased vulnerability also implies that both deterrence and coercion can be more readily enforced. Although major wars may have become less likely, the human penchant for conflict has not waned. Wars will probably remain limited and the concept of conflict also has altered. With increase in economic and military disparities, and unipolarism, terrorism can only increase. The essence was captured by Martin Luther King Jr when he said that "true peace is not merely the absence of terrorism, it is the presence of justice." Ours is an imperfect world. There can be many interpretations of justice, but it is the perceived lack of capability to counter exploitation that results in terrorism. There will always be exploitation and hence terrorism will continue to plague us. Unfortunately, terrorism cannot be contained and has no borders. Probably even more unfortunately, the 11 Sep 2001 attacks on the World Trade Centre and the Pentagon, the wars that followed, and the still continuing insecurity in Afghanistan and Iraq, have given a fillip to international terrorism.

One other aspect that has changed our security scene is the nuclear capability overtly demonstrated by India and Pakistan in May 1998. The non-proliferation regime is at pains to stop any further proliferation. The carrots offered include rewards of varying nature including economic support and transfer of hi-tech capabilities etc. At the same time, more and more stringent measures are being introduced to police the world to prevent proliferation. It is a moot point if such measures can succeed as long as self-interest remains the guiding and overriding principle, and policies change with time. Also, the advertised possible use of nuclear weapons in war cannot but give a fillip to proliferation, at least attempted proliferation.

The few aforementioned changes have certainly altered the manner in which we should perceive conflict and its possible resolution. However, of still greater importance is that the pace of change is forever accelerating. We must learn to forecast the direction of the changes, identify their occurrence, speedily understand their significance, and have the mental capacity to manage the change. All this is easier said than done, but it would be instructive to examine the expected nature of conflict, and the nature of terrorism and how to combat it. An attempt to crystal gaze at what the future holds should also be in order.

Expected Nature of Conflict

The 1648 Treaty of Westphalia recognised the sovereignty of the nation state as the basis of world order. It was assumed that sovereignty implied the freedom to do what you like in your own country. The concept is no longer valid. Interdependence and creation of multilateral organisations has ensured that some bit of sovereignty has had to be sacrificed for the common good. This also implies that states have a stake in the condition and functioning of other states. Some would go so far as to suggest that they have the 'right' to consider resorting to pre-emption if considered necessary.

It was in 1837 that the then US Secretary of State Daniel Webster stated that military pre-emption was valid only if the threat was real and immediate, there were no other options that could be examined, and there was no time available to explore other means towards a peaceful resolution of the discord. However history records any number of instances, well before Gulf War II, where military pre-emption was exercised without cause. In fact, the term has been part of the military lexicon for a long time. Gulf War II is only the most celebrated example, and could well act as a precedent that could make pre-emption more frequent and more acceptable, particularly if it happens in someone else's country!

Military pre-emption resulting in a major war is possible only when the protagonist is strong enough to withstand international pressures. Even then, annexation of territory resulting from a military victory is unlikely to be accepted. Under these circumstances, lies the purpose of the armed forces.

Purpose of the Armed Forces

The primary purpose of the armed forces is to deter any aggression. This is best achieved by having the capability to withstand an attack, and to deny any military victory. The other purpose is coercion, implying the threat of use of force to compel the adversary to accede to our demands. If world opinion will permit only a limited war — limited in terms of geographical area, war objectives, duration, and forces employed— the actual use of forces is less important than the ability to deter and coerce. Deterrence and coercion should be viewed as instruments of policy, with diplomacy backed by credible coercive threats. In other words, military might is required to exercise the needed psychological pressure. The psychological pressure cannot be in place unless the adversary is convinced of our resolve to use military power as appropriate. Use of the armed forces in the recent past, in Kargil and then during Operation Parakaram, did not exhibit resolve as we could and should have.

India is now a nuclear power but sworn to no first use, and no use against any state that does not have any WMDs. Against both China and Pakistan, we have a viable second-strike capability and vice versa. Hence, it is sometimes argued that as the purpose of war is to gain, the losing side is bound to escalate the conflict to avoid losses, and the continued escalation by one side and then the other cannot but result in escalation to a nuclear exchange. Arguments of this type often lead to esoteric discussions on threshold levels, and the entire subject of nuclear war fighting. Such a discussion is indeed far fetched. Nuclear weapons have a deterrent and political role to play. The recent US stand as given in their 2002 National Strategic Security Review, that nuclear weapons may be used for war fighting as opposed to deterrence, is a matter of concern. It is hoped that the US will exercise greater restraint and prudence. The US position is unlikely to have an impact on us. As far as we are concerned, as long as there is no serious asymmetry in the nuclear capabilities with our adversaries, and a mutual credible second-strike capability exists, a stalemate obtains. The deterrent is stable and in place. Even under these circumstances, prudence would suggest that a limited war is sensible only if escalation can be controlled. For this we need greater military power and the ability to exercise it speedily and effectively. At all stages, the adversary should be convinced that any escalation will result in immediate losses that are not commensurate with the likely gains. The point being made will probably be better understood when it is considered that the limited war envisaged could be episodic and sporadic and where the militaries need not even face each other. Air power is ideally suited for such action and to deter escalation. However, required capability has to be created.

Limited wars must be short lived. Hence, attrition warfare is history; perseverance and bravery belong to another age. Brainpower and thought through actions will hold the premium. The military action must be fast paced and effective. The frequency of use of the military will certainly be low, but in this highly competitive world, conflict and the desire to score over the other in the myriad competitive fields, for instance economic development and diplomacy, will always endure. The civil and military aspects of conflict are irrevocably intertwined. Therefore, conflicts will now be both multi-dimensional and continuous.

More so than ever before, the multi-disciplinary nature of conflict has come to stay. Before this, economists decided whether war was affordable, the diplomats and politicians buttressed their cases, and the conduct of war was largely left to the military. This can no longer happen. In fact the salience of military action in conflict resolution is likely to decrease. Economics, diplomacy, media, political compulsions will fashion national objectives and will have a mutually supporting role to play with the armed forces. They will have a continuous impact on military operations both in terms of planning and actual utilisation. Also, the strengths and weaknesses of the military will have an important impact on the other disciplines. Joint decisions, based on varied and diverse inputs, must be the norm in the planning, equipping and conduct of operations.

We have to learn to live v ith the more insidious nature of continuous conflict. Such conflict cannot have an end. The relationship with different countries will remain in a state of flux. The *status quoists* will become less popular. On our part we should aim to adopt a slow and gradual process with the aim to progressively contain a problem, or slowly but surely further our interests. This can briefly be stated as follows:

1. Our armed forces must be designed and equipped to be an effective deterrent against attacks on us, able to exercise needed coercion in conjunction with diplomacy, and pose as a viable force to fight and win in case deterrence, coercion, and compellence fail. At the same time, given international sensibilities, force should be used discriminately in order to ensure that deterrence is speedily reinforced and diplomacy not undermined.
2. Major or cataclysmic wars are unlikely. The costs of war, both economically and for good international relations, are becoming prohibitive. Annexation of territories is a taboo. The concept of victory has changed to one of success in furthering diplomatic and political objectives.
3. Limited wars can and will occur. Escalation dominance is the key to ensure that military actions do not get out of hand.
4. Attrition warfare is history. Sheer bravery and perseverance belong to another age.
5. Military conflicts will be fast paced and time sensitive.
6. The planning and prosecution of conflict has to be multidimensional. The continuous nature of conflict makes this inevitable. Military actions have to be in consonance with political objectives and constraints.

7. Nuclear war is unlikely.
8. Terrorism will remain an endemic plague.

Terrorism and Counter Terrorism

The essence of terrorism was well captured by Martin Luther King Jr. when he said that "true peace is not merely the absence of terrorism but the presence of justice. It is the perceived exploitation and inability to seek justice that breeds terrorism. Once the breeding ground is fertile, and the movement gathers steam, the movement takes on a political colour. Thereafter it becomes increasingly difficult to combat and control the problem. National and International systems are supposedly based on the rule of law, but are the laws always justly and equitably applied? The answer to the question is often in doubt. Often the laws, made by the strong, are applied in the interest of the strong in order to at least perpetuate if not increase their power. The NPT and other non-proliferation regimes are a good case in point. It can also be taken for granted that, human nature being what it is exploitation will remain endemic. Therefore, terrorism in one form or the other will continue to plague us. Organisations like Al Qaeda are unlikely to disappear. Terrorism also transcends national borders and terrorism anywhere should be viewed as terrorism everywhere. However, in spite of UNSCR 1373, a concerted international action to quell terrorism is unlikely. This is particularly so as terrorism is often supported in other countries by some states in order to further their own interests. Pakistan supported terrorism in our country is one such example. Given individual state perceptions and compulsions, we must learn to deal with the menace on our own.

Terrorist organisations are becoming more powerful. The menace is arguably the most dangerous threat facing us and dealing with it is our greatest challenge. The nature of terrorist activities is also changing and becoming more sophisticated. The scope and scale of activities is increasing; better equipment is being provided, often superior to that fielded by anti-terrorist state units. More funding is also available. The terrorists are now able to combine and unholy mix of audacity, ruthlessness, resolve and extended reach. Intense propaganda is resorted to and advantage is taken of the media penchant for sensationalism.

The suicide bombers represent yet another potent threat. They are seemingly undeterred by death. If they have any fear at all, it is the fear of failure. The terrorists deliberately operate near residential areas so that action by state forces is considerably hampered. An unpalatable choice is presented — the choice of *de facto* recognition of the terrorist movement, or of risking the lives of non-combatants causing collateral damage, and maybe even a political backlash. Many other novel means will be thought of in time. Terrorism has indeed been raised from the tactical to the strategic level.

Terrorism and insurgencies in India are menacing problems that will not go away. High levels of terrorist activities obtain in J&K and in the North-East. The Maoists are growing and now cover a corridor from Andhra Pradesh to Nepal. We are also ringed with neighbours equally plagued with insurgencies. In spite of this, the neighbours provide sanctuaries to terrorists that operate in India. Unfortunately, we are constrained, as we are prisoners of our democratic values and our international reputation as a peace-loving state that is not interventionist. Hence, we can adopt only a limited military posture.

Good governance, better routine administration, equitably applied rule of law and control of migration into our country will certainly ease the problem. This aspect of the cure has always been within our grasp, but has eluded us to a large extent. Again, economic development will ease the support given to the terrorists in our country, but economic progress of the entire region is probably the most important measure to curb terrorism in India and in our neighbourhood. Otherwise, our neighbours will have their own geo-strategic imperatives, and maybe, view our progress with some trepidation and as a threat from an emerging hegemonistic power. Our growing role in the world will be acceptable and supported by our neighbours if we help them grow as well and create economic interdependence so that all countries have a stake in maintaining peace and harmony.

The military has a role to play in curbing terrorism. However, as the populace is less willing to accept casualties, there are increasing constraints in the use of force. Great discrimination has to be applied, missions carefully chosen, and only precision attacks undertaken. The media should also be used to advertise the high handedness of the terrorists, and the dangers of aiding or trusting them.

The advances in technology have to be harnessed to produce new and novel means to deal with the problem. Use of non-lethal weapons should be explored. Above all, we must give greater impetus and funding for 'intelligence' activities. Good intelligence will always be the bedrock of a viable counter terrorist strategy. The armed forces would also be well advised to revise their doctrine in the light of new forms of conflict. A different mix of aims and objectives, equipments needed, training requirements, and changed mindsets should form part of the new doctrine.

The Future with a Stark Choice

In the last decade, we have been witness to some phenomenal changes. It can be stated with confidence that the changes likely to occur in the coming years will be equally if not more momentous. The pace of change is also accelerating. It is a stark choice that faces us. Either we speedily learn to adapt with the changing times, or get left behind. The 'status quoists' are behind times. The large moneys being spent on research in space, biotechnology, information technology, more effective weapon systems etc. indicates that major transformations are afoot that will significantly alter power equations. We must do whatever is needed to ensure that we are part of the group of countries that shape the world order in one way or another. Our penchant for adopting principled stands may have to be offset by practical realism even if it is somewhat irksome to our sensibilities. In this respect we should seriously consider increasing our participation in global efforts at nuclear non-proliferation, fight against terrorism, and UN Peace Keeping Operations as well as Peace Enforcing Operations under Chapter VII of the UN Charter.

With terrorism and nuclear proliferation very much part of our lives, and astounding space capabilities and sophisticated information warfare on the cards, the spectrum of conflict has enlarged. In the military sphere we should be ready to face challenges starting from a major war to sub-conventional warfare. For greater investments in more productive avenues, defence budgets have to be kept limited. In spite of this, we have to fashion a military force that is more than capable to meet the more likely demands, and is adequate to thwart enemy designs in other contingencies that may occur. A well thought out long-term plan is required. Maybe it is time that we create well integrated, adaptable, multi-purpose forces that can be readily modified depending on mission requirements. We also need to invest much more in training, in all meanings of the word.

A recent SIPRI (Stockholh International Peace Research Institute) report says that in the past decade. of 118 conflicts, only 10 or so have been inter-state. These are telling figures as to the expected nature of military conflicts. Possibly more importantly, it has become difficult to clearly differentiate between inter-state and intra-state conflict. The domestic, inter-state, and global dimensions of conflict are more intertwined than ever before. The armed forces may also have to contend with mission statements that are not really clear, explicit and coherent; and may also have to operate under conditions of debilitating constraints. We also have to learn to manage uncertainties.

Conclusion

In the fast changing paradigm of security, the first and cardinal requirement is that we cannot allow mindsets to inhibit the acceptance of change. Thereafter we must be able to adapt to the altered realities. All this has to happen speedily and irrevocably.

There are a range of scenarios that can be painted, including military scenarios, but the essential need is for rapid action and reaction to eventualities. A more proactive role is also envisaged. Mental mobility, mental acuity, and mental agility must guide our actions. A good yardstick to measure our standing is the extent to which we can modernise our thoughts, procedures and capabilities. That said, the crucial need for 'intelligence information' in all disciplines cannot be over emphasized. We must have adequate information, properly processed and analysed, and disseminated as and when required.

With the ongoing multi-dimensional nature of continuous conflict, a fundamental transformation in civil-military relationship and interaction has also become inevitable. This transformation must happen in spite of serious policy, political and bureaucratic hurdles. It should be recognised as a prerequisite for an effective deterrent and coercive diplomacy.

7

Internal Security Parameters — Need For Fresh Thinking

Lt Gen (Retd.) Vijay Oberoi

Introduction

India faces many internal challenges, as it attempts to progress and seeks to gain a rightful place in regional and world affairs. There are basically four root causes for internal threats. These are sub-regional aspirations, weak-governance; systemic corruption; and a social and financial divide. They lead to disruptive conditions or internal threats, like armed violence, militancy, insurgency, terrorism, ethnic dissonance, disruption of governance and law and order, and so on. High levels of internal turbulence attract external threats of one kind or another. Disruptive internal conditions also bring down the 'capacity' and the 'will' to tackle external challenges.

Need to Evolve Effective Strategies

Internal conflicts usually emanate from socio-political, ethnic and economic causes, and hence their resolution also lies in the political domain. Unfortunately, in India, they tend to be viewed as exclusive security issues and the major factors, like socio-political and developmental aspects are ignored or are relegated to lower priorities. There is certainly a need to evolve holistic, pragmatic and effective strategies and structures for tackling internal security situations and not rely solely or in the main, on managing such conflicts by use of force. Force may be necessary, in varying degrees, but it is patently wrong to assume that force alone will sort out such problems. There is a definite need for a synergetic approach for the management of high-grade internal conflicts, like insurgency, terrorism and proxy war.

Internal conflicts can broadly be classified in three categories. These are politico-military, quasi-military and non-military. The first two have security connotations, as the names imply, while the third falls in the administrative domain. In my presentation today, I will touch only on the politico-military and quasi-military categories. Most internal security situations are likely to fall in the quasi-military category, but some extreme cases fall in the politico-military category too. For example, the proxy war in J&K, initiated by Pakistan, does require military force to tackle it and thus falls in the military category. Let me, however, hasten to add that conflict management or conflict resolution of internal conflicts has to be a holistic affair, where all instruments and institutions of the state have to work together in a synergistic manner for the common goal.

The instruments available to tackle internal conflicts of the quasi-military category, besides political and administrative, are the various types of state and central police forces, and paramilitary forces. The Army should only be employed as a last resort in exceptional circumstances.

Our country has been inflicted with internal conflicts of many types, practically from the time we became independent. The Army has invariably found itself involved in most of these, as the police forces of the states as well as the central government are unable to control them. The Army has been dealing with the Naga insurgency for nearly five decades and even today a substantial force is deployed in the affected areas, although a cease-fire is in place and negotiations are continuing to resolve the conflict peacefully. The Army has been and continues to be deployed for tackling various insurgency situations in practically all our states in the North-East. In the eighties and nineties, a large part of the Army was deployed in Punjab to tackle the Sikh insurgents, who at the behest of and with the full support of Pakistan, had let loose a reign of terror in Punjab. Fortunately, with the active assistance of the people of Punjab, the insurgency and terrorism were brought to an end, by relentless operations of the Army and the police.

Since 1989, the Army, along with a variety of police forces, are carrying out large-scale operations in the state of Jammu & Kashmir, to tackle insurgency, terrorism and proxy war unleashed by Pakistan, using both indigenous and foreign insurgents and totally backed, in all respects, by Pakistan. A large part of the Army is employed to tackle this internal conflict in the state of Jammu & Kashmir.

Assam Rifles, an efficient paramilitary force, operating under the direct control of the Army, has been operating alongside the Army in all the North-Eastern States for fighting insurgents. At the height of insurgency in Punjab, a new force, the Rashtriya Rifles was raised. Although called a paramilitary force, it was essentially an extension of the Army, as it was fully manned, trained, equipped and officered by the Army. For various reasons, only a few units of this force were raised for fighting the Punjab insurgency. Later, when insurgency in the state of J & K escalated, more units of the Rashtriya Rifles were raised and deployed in J & K. Today, the Rashtriya Rifles has a large number of formation headquarters and units and it is operating effectively against the insurgents and terrorists in J & K.

The roles of the Army are quite clear. Its primary role is to fight external aggression. It is essentially for this that the nation pays to maintain an Army, as well as the other Services. The Army has some secondary roles too. These are assistance to the civil authorities in the maintenance of law and order, when it is beyond the capability of the civil administration, including the police forces; assistance in the maintenance of essential services; and assistance during natural and other calamities. The caveat here is that the secondary role must never dilute the ability of the Army to perform its primary role.

Since Independence, the Army has been used on numerous occasions to come to the assistance of the populace, during riots and other internal disturbances, as also to provide succour in natural and man-made calamities. Although the excessive use of the Army in such duties has an adverse effect on the combat potential of the Army, it is undoubtedly a fact that the Army has endeared itself to the people on account of its impartiality, discipline and above all, effectiveness. It has become a truism that when everyone fails, it is only the Army that delivers. But all this comes at a heavy price. Excessive involvement of the Army in internal security duties adversely affects the combat potential of the Army. Despite being an apolitical force, the Army, when employed in internal security duties tends to be identified, wrongly no doubt, with different political groups by different factions involved in spreading mayhem and chaos. Continued employment of the Army on such duties also tends to alienate the populace and tarnishes the image of the Army. Therefore, over-exposure of the Army in internal security duties is counter-productive, especially when their employment on such duties is for a prolonged period.

Although there has been an exponential growth of many types of police forces in our country, they are currently incapable, or unwilling, or both, to tackle insurgencies. Consequently, the Army will continue to be called out to tackle insurgencies, terrorism, proxy wars and even high-grade internal security situations. We need to change this. The Army's many suggestions for upgrading the professionalism and efficiency of the police forces have unfortunately been glossed over by the political, bureaucratic and police leadership.

As the police forces are still not capable of handling high-grade insurgency situations and the employment of the Army has adverse implications, a separate force within the army, which may be named Internal Security Force (ISF), tasked to fight insurgencies, terrorism and proxy war, would be able to meet the requirement. This would result in the Army still being the 'lead force' in tackling high-grade internal conflicts, but at the same time there will be no dilution of the combat potential and the conventional capability of the regular army. Rashtriya Rifles and Assam Rifles already provide the kernel for building up such a force, which must be a part of the Army, *albeit* distinctly separate in its roles and duties.

Internal conflicts need to be managed by available forces in a tiered manner, so that appropriate force is used, depending on the gravity of the situation. The following tiers are suggested:—

> First Tier. Local police for low level law and order situations.
>
> Second Tier. State armed police for upgraded internal security situations, which are beyond the capability of the local police.
>
> Third Tier. Central police forces for high-level internal security situations and low-level insurgency.
>
> Fourth Tier. The Internal Security Force (ISF) of the Army for counter-insurgency, terrorism and proxy-war situations.

The ISF should be an integral part of the Army and should be deployed, employed and controlled by Army Headquarters, through the appropriate command headquarters and other formation headquarters, as is relevant.

The resolution of internal conflicts essentially lies in the political domain. The security forces do have a role, an important role, and that is to bring down the levels of terrorism and insurgency, so that the political process can re-start. But the key to success in all types of internal security and insurgency situations is good governance and socio-economic development. These may get temporarily disrupted on account of the actions of the insurgents and terrorists, but the game plan must always be to restart these at the earliest.

Intelligence Factor

Intelligence is perhaps the single-most important factor in conducting successful operations against insurgents. All intelligence gathering agencies should therefore be placed under the highest headquarters of the force employed in tackling the situation. Our past and even current experience in this regard has unfortunately been much less than desirable. It is essential that in situations of high grade insurgency, terrorism and proxy war, we do away with routine bureaucratic systems and hierarchies, otherwise we will not be able to tackle these major problems optimally.

Let me now touch on two important issues viz. 'unity of effort' and 'close coordination'. Both are essential if we want to, firstly manage and thereafter resolve, these types of internal conflicts. 'Unity of effort' implies coordinated government effort and unified planning by all instruments of the state. In addition, centralised control is essential. There must also be clear-cut responsibility and accountability. Lastly, there has to be intimate cooperation between the civil officials and the uniformed forces.

Coordination can be best achieved if all organs of the state work in unison. Nominating a security adviser and arming him with maximum powers best achieves the coordination of all security forces. Up to Tier-3, the Adviser could be the DG Police. In case, insurgency is being tackled at the Tier-4 level, the Adviser should be the Army or Corps commander. But it is not just the security forces that need to coordinate their efforts. There is also a need for coordinating organisations based on a number of committees, down to district and tehsil levels. The following committees would be useful: -

- State Council. The Chief Minister should chair this. Its members should be selected ministers, the Security Adviser and the Chief Secretary. It should lay down policy and identify macro level thrust areas.
- State Coordination Committee. The Chief Secretary could be the chairperson, with members being the Security Adviser, the Home Secretary, Secretaries of relevant departments, like law, finance, development, public relations, education and health. Other secretaries may be co-opted on an as required basis. The other members should be the commanders of military and paramilitary forces, and the DG Police of the state. This committee would translate the directions laid down by the State Council into implementable plans.

State Operational and Intelligence Coordination Committee. The chairperson should be the commander of the Internal Security Force (ISF) and the members should be the commanders of all police forces as well as all intelligence organisations.

District Coordination Committees. The senior ISF commander and the Deputy Commissioner (DC) should jointly chair these.

- Need-based Committees. These could be State Intelligence Coordination Committee or State Public Information and Counter Propaganda Committee.

Conclusion

In sum, let me state that internal threats, which have security overtones can be managed and in time resolved, provided we approach the problem in a holistic manner. These are political and socio-economic problems and therefore their resolution also lies in the political, cultural and developmental domains. We must not treat them as just security or law and order problems, and rely on the use of force to solve them, as we have done in the past and continue to do even now.

8

How Secured is India? Destabilising Factors

P. C. Dogra

Introduction

Traditionally, when we talk of national security, it is the security from an external threat. The total emphasis is on the borders with our neighbours. Now it is an obsolete idea. This view needs to be re-oriented. One does not have to go to war to break up the country. Internal subversion in such a diverse country like India will do the needful. Even if you are suffering an incalculable loss in terms of human lives and financially because of the proxy war unleashed by a hostile neighbour, international community will not let you go to war to teach your recalcitrant neighbour a lesson. Mobilisation of the Indian army after the terrorist attack on our Parliament on 13 Dec. 2002 and thereafter demobilisation after about eight months without firing a single shot under the pressure of international community, clearly shows the compulsions of the Govt. of India, shows inability of our nation to resort to conventional war under lurking apprehension of a nuclear retaliation. Even the limited war option to get quick results in the context of a terrorist attack on Parliament could not also be contemplated. Stephen P. Cohen, a renowned expert on South Asia in his address to the U.S. Senate Committee on Foreign Relations had observed, "There are senior officers (in India) who advocate 'limited war' to teach Pakistan a lesson. The 2002 crisis was a turning point: Indian Generals could not promise that a limited war against Pakistan would not go 'nuclear' and the political leadership concluded that the risks of such a war were too great"

Even during Kargil war, when Pakistani forces had intruded into our territory, inspite of the strategic imperatives of crossing the LoC and encircling the enemy from behind, it was not resorted to and we never crossed the LoC though we had to pay a very heavy price in men and materials. We may also refer to Hussain Haqqani's book 'Pakistan between Mosque and Military', wherein he says that "Pakistan military had prepared nuclear tipped missiles to repulse a possible Indian attack during Kargil crisis". It has encouraged our neighbour to continue sponsoring subversive activities in our country without any let up and with impunity by resorting to nuclear blackmail. So it has become imperative that we give unequivocal attention to the internal security of nation while at the same time ensuring the inviolability and the sanctity of our borders. It is not a boundary dispute with China as it is not the Kashmir dispute with Pakistan that if and when solved will ease the border tension. It is much bigger game of encircling India and not let it emerge as the world power.

Role of Pakistan

Hussain Haqqani[1] has said that soon after independence "Islamic Pakistan was defining itself through the prism of resistance to Hindu India. Islamist groups have been sponsored and supported by the state machinery. In the South Asia region, they have been allies in the Pakistan's military's efforts to seek strategic depth in Afghanistan and to put pressure on India for negotiations over the future of Kashmir". President Ayub Khan characterised India as a Hindu state and of Hindus as irreconcilable enemies of Islam and Muslims. He was a firm believer in the policy tripod developed within the first few years of Pakistan's creation i.e. India as Pakistan's eternal enemy, Islam as a national unifier and the United States as the country's provider of arms and finances.

As observed by J. N. Dixit, the then National Security Advisor, "The framework of Pakistan's principles and intentions towards India", reflected in the official stance, are the following:

> Pakistan's destiny of emerging as the most important power in South Asia.
>
> India must fragment itself into smaller states, which can be played off one against the other. It also validates the two nation theory.
>
> For this, capture Kashmir and separate North-Eastern India from Indian Republic. Similarly for Punjab.
>
> Pakistan's nuclear capability is to put India on the defensive and offset its conventional military superiority.
>
> With fragmentation of India, there will be a demographic Muslim fragmentation with Muslims looking up to Pakistan as a strong nation for their support."

Amir Taheri, Editor of France's leading journal the *Politique Internationale* has said: "Pakistan's struggle for identity requires in its own analysis of itself, to pursue conflict with India, not rapproachment. Thus the Kashmir conflict will drag on because of its survival and identity as a nation and the theory that created and underpins it." After the Agra Summit, Pervez Musharraf gave a private assessment to his inner circle on the Indian political leadership which he perceived as " indecisive and lacking in unity and further said that the Indian Armed Forces, though adequately equipped are not backed by an assertive political will and, therefore its morale is not high." He also came to the conclusion that, "if a war occurs, Pakistan could certainly match if not defeat India." Pakistan has about 100,000 to 150,000 battle hardened *Jihadis*. But they are only half of those graduated from 29 training camps. According to the Pak Generals, "Kashmir or nothing. Pakistan has no fallback position." They are of the view that India was fast cracking up. Another observation is "Pakistan remains a fragile and restless society in which support for a decade-long guerilla campaign in Kashmir is the only unifying force."

Lt. General Hamid Gul, former ISI Chief said, "keeping the Indian army occupied in internal security amounts to Pakistan having two additional divisions at no extra cost." As per conservative estimates, approximately 46000 tonnes of narcotics pass through Pakistan every year. In terms of money, it generates about $ 8 billion annually. The share of ISI every year is $ 3 billion, an amount more than enough to fund the cross-border terrorism. Nawaz Shrief, Ex Prime Minister of Pakistan, once told the *Washington Post* that in 1990, the then Army Chief General Aslam Beg and the I.S.I Chief had come out with a plan to pay for Pakistan's covert military operations through heroin trafficking. The Afghan war was bank-rolled in this manner.

Now a word about Al Qaeda. It believes in the supra-national, homogenous society organised according to Koranic law. "Modern Nation State is completely antithetical to the Islamic way of life." Islam offering one world state based on religion threatens the existing International order. It has reportedly been estimated by the experts of the monitoring committee of the UN Security Council, which oversees the implementation of UNSC Resolution No. 1373 that despite the freezing/seizing of terrorist funds and other assets worth US $ 112 million since 9/11, Al Qaeda and its allies in the International Islamic Front still have at their disposal about US $ 300 million. Replenishments continue to flow into their funds. In Nov. 2001, during the first phase of *Operation Enduring Freedom*, US military officials discovered in a safe house in Kabul details of meetings between scientists of A. Q. Khan laboratories including Sultan Bashiruddin Mahmood and several Al Qaeda functionaries like Osama himself and Al-Zawahiri. The discovery was said to be so alarming that CIA Director George Tenet immediately rushed to Islamabad to investigate.

Dr Mahmood admitted in questioning that he had held meetings with bin Laden in August 2001 and on the fateful morning of Sept.11 and that he discussed the benefits of an atomic blast in an American city. But he said he only provided academic answers and no technical assistance. However, Dr.

Mahmood was put to six lie detector tests. He failed all. The interrogations, coupled with the findings from the UTN (Ummah Tameer-E-Nau) Hqrs. seemed to verify for the CIA that Al Qaeda had produced several nuclear weapons from highly enriched uranium and plutonium pellets of the size of the silver dollars. At least one weapon was smuggled before 9/11.

"By 2003, the war on terror was costing the American public $ 4.5 billion a month and the national debt rose to $ 6.8 trillion. Moreover, the loss to travel industry was enormous with airlines companies losing $ 13 billion annually. All this was accomplished by Al Qaeda for a mere pittance of less than $ 500,000."[2]

Pakistan based Pan-Islamic terrorist organisations, which are allied with Osama bin Laden in his International Islamic Front have been consistent in their long-term strategy directed against India. They look upon J&K as the gateway to India, its liberation being the *first* stage in their *jihad* against India. *Second* will be the liberation of Hyderabad and Junagadh and *final* would be the "liberation" of the Muslims in the rest of India as a prelude to the formation of an Islamic Caliphate in South Asia.

Youseff Bodansky, Director of US Congressional Task Force on terrorism has mentioned in his book "*Bin Laden: The man who declared war on America*" that bin Laden and the ISI had struck a deal under which the so-called Mujahideen would carry out spectacular terrorist strikes in India and that he has set up major cells in the southern cities of Bangalore and Hyderabad.[3] Again according to Rohen Gunaratna, an expert on Asian terrorist groups at the Centre for the Study of Terrorism and Political violence in USA, "It is only a matter of time before Al Qaeda fully targets India: right now, a few of their operations in India have been disrupted."

It is now confirmed that the six major fires in the ammunition depots of the Indian Army since April 2000 were all acts of sabotage. One Manoj Srivastava, a Pak spy arrested in Calcutta by the security agencies, confessed about the involvement of ISI in these fires.

According to the report of the Group of Ministers on National Security, headed by the then Deputy Prime Minister and Home Minister of India, Sh. L. K. Advani "*Pakistan would continue to pose threat to India's security with a single mindedness of destabilising India, not just focussed on Kashmir but on a search of parity.*"

That this proxy war will never come to an end is amply proved by what General Pervez Musharraf told his officers in 1999, "*even if the Kashmir dispute is resolved, our problems with India may not end, because India wants to keep Pakistan weak, Pakistan is a thorn in India's side, constantly thwarting India's ambition to become a world power.*"

Internal Security

The concept of Internal Security has now acquired multifaceted proportions. It is not only a police surveillance of the possible terrorists but encompasses the monitoring of the various other institutions of the country especially banking and other financial services. Before the Black Tuesday tragedy, nobody had thought of the aircrafts fully loaded with the passengers being hijacked and then hit against the intended targets. Chairman of a House sub-committee on National Security of America has stated, " I am absolutely convinced, we will have a chemical, biological or nuclear attack. The question is not if, it is when, where and what will be the magnitude". White House office estimated in 1993 that an Anthrax release in the Nation's capital could kill as many as 3 million people. As per the report of International Atomic Energy Agency," the world's plutonium reprocessing inventories annually include or exclude scores of kilos of "material unaccounted for", making it possible to clandestinely fabricate a few atomic weapons and it may not be difficult for an organisation like Al Qaeda to procure one. Weapons made of certain material like ceramic or carbon fiber could pass through the X-ray screening un-noticed. One can now visualise a future terrorist carrying a nuclear bomb in the suitcase or a hijacked plane being used to throw anthrax at the inhabited areas.

Pakistan is carrying out its strategic war of inflicting thousand cuts on India. It was launched on a very big scale first in Punjab where the arms/explosives and ammunition recovered from the terrorists could have equipped at least one division of the Indian Army. Can one imagine the quantum of depolyment of the security forces? About four Divisions of the Army were deployed. The two Corps Headquarters were coordinating the anti-secessionist operations. Moreover, 730 Companies of para military forces along with 75,000 men of the Punjab Police, 30,000 Home Guards and 30,000 special police officers were deployed. Such a density of security forces could not stop the casualties. About 12 thousand civilians lost their lives in this mindless violence. The terrorists killed two thousand policemen and their four hundred family members. In return, 8 thousand terrorists were killed and about 21 thousand were arrested.

Now it has been unleashed in the Kashmir valley. Between 1990 and July 2001(upto date information would be just deadly), over 21,000 innocent civilians have been killed in J&K while another 26,000 have been injured. Besides, 3050 security personnel and 13,400 militants have been killed. Mind boggling recoveries have been made from the terrorists operating in the valley, which up to Oct. 2000 were Assault rifles—19,841, Machine guns—1,083, Rocket launchers—1,272, Sniper rifles—295, Mortars—40, Anti-aircraft gun—1, Missile launchers—4, Mines—5,120, indigenous explosive devices—3,278, RDX Explosives—21,689 Kgs.

Other Under Cover Operations of ISI

Some time back, I.G.P/Economic Offences in a report submitted to the U. P. State Hqrs, had evaluated the smuggling of the Indian fake currency to the tune of staggering Rs 1,500 crores from the Indo-Nepal border in addition to the smuggling of the sophisticated fire arms. D-Company runs overt or covert business in over a dozen countries. Annual turnover is estimated at over Rs. 7,000 crores. Reportedly Dawood Ibrahim had some time back donated Rs. 1,000 crores to Musharraf to tide over Pakistan's domestic crisis.

At the high level meeting taken by the then Cabinet Secretary T. S. R. Prasad, it was revealed by the Intelligence Bureau and RBI that at least 25 banks run the risk of harbouring ISI influenced depositors.

Vulnerable Polity of the Indian Nation

Andre Beteille, a renowned sociologist and professor at the Delhi School of Economics says, "No matter what the Indian State and the Govt. would have us believe, the truth is that today the idea of secularism is very negatively connected with community bonding and power acquisition." This, says Beteilli, coupled with law and order machinery prone to political interference is at the root of the social problems, we as a nation face today. One politician aptly remarked. " Electoral politics is determined by what the people want; Not what is good for the people." Just as there is a majority communalism, there is also a minority communalism. Regional leaders float different political parties, catering to the aspirations of the particular caste which itself being in a sizeable number could in alliance with some other group again based on the caste/community permutations could manage to get some seats so as to be in a good position to bargain. VP Singh's OBC card came out only after a threat from Devi Lal emerged. Mulayam Singh Yadav phenomenon has come about entirely because of the Babri/Ayodhya issue.

Madrassas have sprung up in J&K and all over the country specifically along the Indo-Pak border of Punjab, Rajasthan and the Indo-Nepal border with a design to wean Indian Muslims from their traditional Indo-Islamic roots and inculcate in them the philosophy of pan-Islamic fundamentalism. As per the survey carried out by one agency, there are about 42,000 Madrassas operating in the country with one lakh and forty thousands teachers and about 32 lakhs students. In India, Madrassa system of education is modeled on Dars-I-Nizamia which was formulated in the times of Emperor Aurangzeb.[4] The main focus is on the studies on Quran, the Hadis and Fiqah, the objective being to turn out maulvis who prove to be rather fanatic. Talibans as we know were the products of Madrassas in Pakistan.

N.N.Vohra Committee concluded that "The network of the mafia is virtually running a parallel Govt. pushing the state apparatus into irrelevance". It discloses a powerful nexus between the bureaucracy and the politicians with mafia gangs, smugglers and the underworld."

Illegal Migration of Bangladeshis: As regard Indo-Bangladesh border and insurgency in North-East, estimates are that fifteen to twenty million Bangladeshis have migrated to India and are illegal residents. The presence of 15% of another country's population in India underscores a strong negative impact on our national sovereignty. Leftist intellectuals of Bangladesh have demanded lebensraum— living space — for their country's excess population. As many as 55 lakhs ration cards have been issued to Bangladeshis in West Bengal. Illegal Migrants Determination Tribunals Act (IMDT), 1983 is an effective protective shield for the illegal migrants because in Assam under this Act, it is the job of the Police to prove that a particular individual is a foreigner whereas under the Foreigners Act, applicable in the rest of India, the onus is on the illegal migrant to prove that he is an Indian national. It has since been set aside by the Supreme Court. Separation of the North-Eastern areas from India has been the strategic objective of Pakistan since its creation. "According to the official figures" between 1962 and 1984 before the IMDT Act came into being, more than 300,000 of illegal immigrants were deported from Assam. By contrast during the two decades since then, less than 1,600 illegal immigrants were detected and deported"[5] While quashing this Act, "Supreme Court noted that the Muslim population of Assam witnessed 77.42% growth during two decades between 1971-91 while Hindus grew nearly 41.89%." It said that legislation negated the stringent provision of the Foreigners Act, which lays the onus of establishing the right to stay in the country squarely on a suspected illegal migrant.

According to the views of two eminent personalities. Sh. T.V. Rajeshwar (ex-Governor of West Bengal) and (presently) Governor of Uttar Pradesh who has said that " there is a distinct danger of another Muslim country, speaking Bengali predominantly, emerging in the eastern part of India in future, at a time when India might find itself weakened politically and militarily". Lt

General, S.K.Sinha, ex-Governor of Assam and presently Governor of J & K has observed: As important as the Kashmir dispute is the one involving influx of Bangladeshis in the North-East, for this might lead to a demand for the merger of North-East, border areas with Bangladesh and ultimately could create a situation when Dhaka will cut off the region from the rest of the country."

Amanul Haq Chowdhury, Mohammed Ali Jinnah's private secretary, who remained in Assam and later became Minister in Assam Govt, wrote to Jinnah in 1947: "Quad-e-Azam, wait for next thirty years, I shall present Assam to Pakistan in a platter". Because of unchecked illegal migration of Bangladeshis, today out of total of 24 districts of Assam, six districts namely Nagaon, Goalpara, Dhubri, Karim Ganj, Barpeta and Hailakandi have 60% Muslims while other six i.e. Bongaigaon, Kokrajhar, Kamrup, Nalbari, Darang and Cachar districts have above 40% Muslim population. In Nagaland, Dimapur has become a den of Bangladeshis, Kohima has become their second biggest haven. As per the report of the National Minority Commission on 2001 census:

> Nineteen districts in three border states of Assam, West Bengal and Bihar have recorded a 'disproportionate' growth of Muslims over the past decade.
>
> Ten districts of Assam bordering Bangladesh have now a substantive Muslim population as high as 51%.
>
> The Muslim population's growth during 1991-2001 was 29.5%, higher than the overall of 21.5%.

Insurgency in North-East

In an article in the *Time* magazine, carried from Chittagong, a reporter has said, "Southern Bangladesh has become a haven for hundreds of *Jihadis* on the run understandably since two fundamentalist parties, the Jamat-e-Islami and the Islamic Oikya Jote are part of the electoral alliance led by Prime Minister Khalida Zia. Oikya Jote is known to sympathise with Taliban and Al Qaeda and is linked to the Harkat-ul-Jihad-e-Islami, a terrorist group". All the insurgent outfits specifically the United Liberation

Front of Assam (ULFA) have their hide-outs in Bangladesh. ISI of Pakistan operates from Bangladesh to create and support the anti-national elements in the North-East India.

Insurgent outfits like ULFA, ATTF(All Tripura Tiger Force) and National Socialist Council of Nagaland are running business establishments in Bangladesh. ULFA owns Hotel Surma International (Taj Mahal Road Dhaka), Hotel Mohammadia (Dhaka), Hotel Padma International, Hotel Keya International (Jinda Bazar, Sylhet), Hotel Yamuna (Sylhet), Hotel Vasundhra (Chittagong) and Hotel Raqj King (Pahartali, Chittagong). ULFA is also running business establishments like Usha International (Dhaka), Anirban Garments Ltd (Pahartali Chittagong) and Karachi Garments Industry (Chittagong). Some business establishments are the personal property of Paresh Buruah and Arvind Rajkhhova.

There was a major incident of arms seizure in Chittagong on April 2, 2004 in which a huge consignment of Korean, Italian, Chinese and US made weapons including 690 T56-1 Sub Machine guns, 600 T56-2 Sub Machine guns, 150 T-69 Rocket Launchers in addition to more ancillary arms and ammunition were recovered. *Jane's Intelligence Review* has revealed that "the purchases were financed by a foreign intelligence service seeking to destabilise India's North-East and that the shipment involved ULFA's Military Chief Paresh Barua and NSCN's Chief Procurement Officer, Anthony Shimray.

Manipur People's Liberation Front which is a umbrella organisation formed by the federation of the People's Liberation Army, the United National Liberation Front and PREPAK, the three Meitei dominated insurgent outfits, have said, "the task of safeguarding Manipur's integrity cannot be divorced from the national liberation struggle". MPLF of Manipur recently fought a four day pitched battle against three columns of the BSF — the first such instance in the history of Indian insurgency. The Apunba Loop is the coordinating body of 32 agitating organisations. Satjal i.e. Scientific Defence Cultural Society raised in 1937, under the inspiration of the then Maharaja of Manipur to drive out the British from the Manipuri kingdom, has been revived under a new banner of Universal Friendship Organisation. Some

5,000 members dressed in black and supporting a pony tail assembled to observe Manipur independence day, 24 hours before the Indian Independence Day. Its Chief is Raj Kumar Manisana.

Govt of India is holding talks with NSCN (Nationalist Socialist Council of Nagaland) (Issac-Muivah). But their demand is that "All Naga people should be under a single administration." NSCN(IM) is led by a Tangkhul Naga Th.Muivah. Tangkhul tribals live mainly in Ukhrul and Senapati districsts of Manipur. Muivah has said that Ukhrul is a part of the Naga homeland. "There is no greater or lesser Nagaland, only the land inhabited by Nagas". However, Meitei people of Manipur's valley are against any proposal that takes away land from their state.

Left Wing Extremism

The most backward and poor districts spreading from the border of Bihar with Nepal to Rayalseema Districts of Andhra Pradesh where naxalites are concentrated is addressed as the Compact Revolutionary Zone. A district of Gadchiroli of Maharashtra has already seen its 55 colleagues dead in a fight against the PWG. Andhra alone lost its 500 policemen in the last decade. With the Govt wanting to negotiate with PWG and restraining the police from any action, Andhra has already become a safe haven for the Naxalites and the states like Chattisgarh, Orissa and Maharashtra are expecting increase in their activities. They have used the cease fire in Andhra Pradesh to equip themselves as they have not given up the concept of "armed class war". There is already talk of liberated zone of Dandakaranya. Maoists of Nepal and the PWG have formed Revolutionary International Movement and the bonds between Maoists-PWG and the ULFA are growing and further developing with NDFB, Kamatipur Liberation Organisation.

In July 2001, nine extreme left outfits from Sri Lanka, India, Nepal and Bangladesh floated CCOMPOSA (Coordination Committee of Maoists Parties and Organisations in South Asia). MCC which had confined itself to South and Central Distts of undivided Bihar was tasked by CCOMPOSA to build a Red

Bridge to Nepal. Maoist shelters have reportedly sprung up in Champaran forests. The Dandakaranya, the vast stretch from North Telangana to Chhattisgarh is so much under PWG control that the group is ready to declare it a "liberated zone". The Naxalites want a separate state of Telangana because of their relative strength in the backward Telangana region.

According to the Home Ministry information, naxalite activity is spread over 125 districts in 12 states (Andhra Pradesh, Maharashtra, Orissa, Jharkhand, Madhya Pradesh, Chhatisgarh, Bihar, Uttar Pradesh, West Bengal. Tamil Nadu, Kerala are the latest entries). PWG and Maoist Communist Center of India have merged. Home Ministry has made an interesting observation in a note circulated among the Chief Ministers that "any such re-alignment is likely to impart a qualitative impetus to naxalism that has witnessed a perceptible growth in recent years in the form of extensive militarisation, increasing violence and geographical spread".

On Feb. 6, 2004, a few hundred naxalites laid siege to the District Hqrs of Koraput, brought it to a complete halt for few hours, attacked the district Hqrs complex, successfully raided the district Armoury and looted 500 weapons and several thousands of ammunition. Again on June 23, 2005, over 200 Maoists went on the rampage in East Champaran District of Bihar looting many arms, set a police station on fire, killed three Police men. CPI Maoists have launched a countrywide what they call Tactical Counter Offensive Campaign. They have killed K.C. Surendera Babu, the Police Chief of Mungher District on January 5, 2005.

The Maoist raid on Jehanabad jail on Nov. 13, 2005 shows the increasing fire power of the naxalites. Before the raid, over 600 newly recruited Maoists were trained in arms in the Gurap jungle, near the Bihar-Jharkhand border in the presence of Maoists from Andhra Pradesh. North Bihar shares the longest border with Nepal i.e. 643 kms. and through rivers Gandaki and Kosi and roads, the Maoists from Nepal could always have a link with Maoists in Central and South Bihar Districts, which are well-linked to Maoist-affected Hazaribagh and Giridih areas in Jharkhand. They are in turn connected to Purulia in West Bengal which is linked to Midnapore, the gateway of West Bengal to Orissa and Andhra Pradesh.

It loudly proclaims the militarisation that the largest and most lethal naxalite outfit in the country has achieved and the ability of the CPI Maoist leadership to motivate and train a large number of people as well as carry out a successful attack with meticulous planning like snapping of telephone and power lines, blocking and mining the highways. The naxalites conducted a synchronised attacks on District Jail, District Courts, Police Lines, Police Quarters, District Armoury and a Police Station and it was claimed to be a successful military campaign with strong political overtones. An overwhelming number of ordinary people also participated who can be termed as people's militia. It indicates the intensity of support, which the naxalites have come to cultivate from the general masses. With the public participation getting momentum, it could lead to people encircling towns and ultimately, though a wild imagination, there could be a *Long March* to Delhi.

Maoists have set up a Central Military Commission, which plans, co-ordinates and directs operations from time to time. One such was raid on Home Guards Training center at Giridih near Ranchi on Nov. 11, 2005 which killed five police men, looted 185 weapons and 3,000 bullets.

In an interview[6] given to a correspondent of *Hindustan Times*, senior members of the CPI (Maoists) Central Committee said that they plan to target the companies, including MNCs which are setting up projects by forcibly displacing people. They further said that they also intend to target police armouries to arm tribals along the red corridor—from Nepal to South to fight the displacement. "The Dandakaranya-Vishakhapatnam gas pipeline is a target." Asked about their resources, they did not rule out raids on the banks a shift in their policy—if there was a need to replenish their coffers. "The option of raising it through levies is also open."

India as a Nation is suffering from a seige mentality. Punjab and the Rajasthan borders with Pakistan have been fenced.

Indo-Bangladesh border is being fenced. Any trouble on the border, fence it and feel secured. We are doing the greatest damage to the Nation. We are demolishing the *do or die* instinct of the Nation. What is required is the proactive stance of the Nation as a whole. How long will we keep on fencing ourselves? Reactive counter-insurgency policy involving limited security operations against the militants will not carry us far. We must not take any more beating. Indian leadership across the political spectrum lacks vision. Our leaders are driven by their short-term gains. Every statement of them caters to one electoral constituency or the other. Here the politics is the pursuit of power. There is not an *iota of doubt* that in case of war with Pakistan, there will be a large-scale internal sabotage all over the country.[7] William S. Cohen, a Republican Senator and a Statesman has said, "This potential combination of terrorism and technology is the primary peril facing the world." POTA was enacted by India as a part of the international fight against terrorism. It has now been repealed just to appease the minority vote bank. Recently there was a warning to the Govt. of India from Jaish-e-Mohammed by way of Delhi Bomb explosions of Oct.29, 2005 with funds from Middle East.

We must act in time otherwise it will be too late to hold the country together.

References

1. *Pakistan between Mosque and Military* by Hussain Haqqani.
2. Osama's Revenge : *The Next 9/11* by Paul L. Williams.
3. *Ibid.*
4. *Madrassa Education in India* by Kuldeep Kaur.
5. Article in *Hindustan Times,* July 25, 2005 "Return to Sender."
6. Interview given to Mammen Mathew, *Hindustan Times,* Dec. 14, 2005.
7. William S. Cohen (a Republican Senator), *Hindustan Times,* Nov. 16, 2005.

9

Darkness Under the Thousand Suns: Scanner On Destabilising Forces

Tarun Vijay

Introduction

When the Western scientists were putting Galileo to death for his beliefs, Hindu rishis had discovered that there are not one but many Suns in the cosmic world. Their wisdom and tolerance for a differing view is a unique characteristic of our civilisation. Sadly enough, the land of universal brotherhood and mutual co-existence is facing threats to its own existence today because of Islamic terrorism, intolerant ideologies and a planned population aggression, especially on our border areas. The exterior sources and supporters of these fissiparous and anti national tendencies are *Jihadi Islamists*, extreme leftists active in under the garb of Maoist and the Church supported insurgency in the North-East. This has had a more deadly effect due to the strange *lackadaisical* attitude of the central and state governments in the name of a self-defeating secularism. This situation demands national conscience to be shaken up and reawakened. It seems we have forgotten all the elements that made us resist the enemies for the last thousand years and still keep the flag high, while other nations were simply besmirched under the horses of the Islamists and Christian aggressors. A nation with a thousand year old history of foreign invasions and an invincible spirit of resistance, yet we are so aloof from our immediate security concerns and threats looming large over our head. We, the people of India, fall in the category of *illusionists with a chilling ease.*

Take Himalayas, once calle l the unconquerable security wall of the grand Aryavarta i.e Hindusthan. The myth fell apart in '62 aggression by the Chinese and still neither the younger generation nor the sunset leadership in politics seems to be much bothered about securing the security wall, nature had so thoughtfully gifted us. From J & K to Arunachal, we have Ladakh, Himachal, Uttaranchal, UP and Bihar's border area with Nepal, Sikkim and Assam reaching up to the Tawang region of Arunachal on this belt.

Not a single spot can be said to be a secure and unthreatened one and the fears of disturbance are increasing day by day on this entire belt. While Ladakh, Himachal, Uttaranchal, UP and Bihar are basically threatened by *Islamic Jihadis* and their population aggression with active hub centers in their madrassas, presently joined by the Communist terrorists in the guise of Maoists, the North-Eastern region is rife with Church supported insurgent movements. Many of the border areas in Uttaranchal, Bihar, Arunachal and UP-Nepal belt have shown an extraordinary increase in the Muslim population to the tune of 120% and more. It just cant be brushed aside as a natural phenomenon and needs probe going beyond the religious faultlines. Nation's security should be the highest altar of faith for us.

More than two dozens of fully equipped terrorist organizations working relentlessly for secession in an isolated and ignored masses, yet there is no focus on the education and acculturisation of the people inhabiting remote border areas and almost no special effort to bring these people (specially the younger generation into the national mainstream). It indicates horrendous lack of wisdom to safeguard the geographical and cultural territories of the nation. A few examples from three different parts of the Himalayan belt, which only provide a brief idea about the enormity of the whole problem are given below.

Arunachal: A couple of years back it was known as the only bastion of peace in the troubled North-East. But gradually the forced religious conversions and accompanied insurgency by the National Socialist Council of Nagaland (Issac-Muivah) in Changlang and Tirap districts and lethargic attitude of the centre has brought this beautiful state on the brink of unrest. Arunachal's border with China is a long one, which stretches all the way from its east, over to its northern boundaries and down to its North-Western edge where it merges with Tibet. To its west is Bhutan and on its southern end it touches Assam, Nagaland and Burma before sweeping up to China, which still holds 40,000 square kilometers (besides it also controls 16,000 square mile of Indian Territory in Kashmir). China lays claim to almost entire territory in Arunachal Pradesh. Though the state leadership had risen issues of security from time to time, the Delhi Govt. have chosen not to listen to their whistles.

The following news item will show the concerns of a patriotic leader, which went unheard:

February 15, 2003 (AFP)—*India's remote Northeastern state of Arunachal Pradesh urged the federal government to improve infrastructure along the border with China to meet any security threat from its neighbour. "We need to lay emphasis on constructing vital roads along our borders with China to meet any security threats,"* Chief Minister Mukut Mithi told AFP by telephone from state capital Itanagar on Friday.

The Arunachal Pradesh government has been warning New Delhi about Chinese troops making forays across the border and Mithi said India and China should demarcate borders to prevent any confrontation. "Improving border roads in our territory would not only help in easy movement of troops, but enable trade and commerce between the two countries to flourish."

China has also begun a controversial, 118-kilometre (650-mile) railway project, and the first to link China with Tibet, which can currently be accessed only by air or via tortuous roads. It will stretch from the Tibetan capital Lhasa to Golmud in western China and will be the world's highest railway.

Bhutan: Though Bhutan has helped to flush out terrorist oganisations active from its soil at Indian Govt.'s request, the sheer number of such organisations and their clout is a modest reminder of the gravity of real situation in the North-Eastern states, where virtually Delhi's rule is a limited one now. These are some of the terrorist organizations that were active from Bhutan, as follows:

United Liberation Front of Assam (ULFA)

National Democratic Front of Bodoland (NDFB)

Bodo Liberation Tigers Force (BLTF)

Kamatapur Liberation Organisation (KLO)

Manipur

Manipur too is facing a long drawn battle fully supported by the local church. It is a jewel in the crown of the age-long civilisational body of the nation, surrounded by beautiful lakes, mountains, inhabited by the great dancers and scholars and poets who have influenced the heart and mind of rest of India and taken the fragrance of our cultural garden far and wide around the globe. But now it is burning and the soul of India is in tears. Recently the greatest treasure of the tiny tribal state, a library containing thousands of rare manuscripts and books, dating hundreds of years back, was burnt down. The physical losses ran into several crores of rupees, but the real value can never be calculated, as the national treasure of the rare manuscripts and literature is lost forever.

It was burnt because the local Meitei movement, actively supported by the Communists and the church, wanted the Bengali script to be replaced by Meitei and the library contained books in the Bengali script, because that has been the long time cherished tradition of the state. A couple of months back the Vice-Chancellor of Manipur University was abducted and tortured, because the extremist organisation Kanglei Yayol Kannan

Lup wanted its own man to head the audio-visual research centre at the University. He had, in fact, appointed a person supported by another extremist students organisation, the United National Liberation Front, and was later shot in the leg. None protested, not the faculty nor the students.

In Manipur, National song is banned and is not sung either in schools or any other public platform. Even Manipuri books are not allowed to include it in their pages. In the text book screening committees, set up by the government representatives of separatist organisations like the All Manipur Students Union, the Democratic Students Alliance of Manipur, the Manipur Students Federation (a Maoist outfit) force, the committee to teach only Manipur issues, leaving out of its gambit Gandhi, Nehru and other national heroes. The State Council of Research and Training just cannot say 'no' to these elements.

In a Robin Hood role, student organisations check teachers' conduct and cut their salary if they are found to be absent from classes. The money collected is deposited in their association's account. In the government sector, the Kanglipak Communist Party, the United National Liberation Front and the Kanglei Yayol Kannan Lup are most active and impose a 'tax' which none can refuse. Government employees are forced to give 1 to 2 per cent of their salary and each central project contractor or the officer in charge has to cough up 10 to 20 per cent of the project cost. It is all in the open.

People who have the 'blessings' of the separatist organisations run the show in the offices like gangsters, become the source of all information and guide the 'actions' if needed. The separatist movements have taken root with clear support from Leftist extremist groups and church-inspired elements.

This tendency has further been strengthened by the sheer apathy of the Delhi Sultans, who remain satisfied with their blurred image of a Hindustan, which does not really matter beyond Kolkata in the east.

The last ten years have seen a meticulous consolidation of the separatist forces. The AMSU was formed in 1962 as a genuine students body, which was 'taken over' by the separatist UNLF in 1997. The People's Liberation Army, another insurgent outfit, ended up having a different students body named the Manipur Students Federation (Maoist).

A breakaway group from the UNLF was formed as the KYKL in 1985 which joined hands with the National Socialist Council of Nagaland—Issac-Muivah group (NSCN-IM) who helped it counter the influence of the UNLF, its arch enemy. The KYKL has established its students group, DESAM, having almost total control over Manipur University. Another influential revivalist movement leader revered is Khonangthava who emerged as a powerful reformist in the early 20th century and emphasised Manipur's pre-Vaishnavite traditions.

After great debate and pressure from separatist students organisations, the Vice-Chancellor had to concede their demand to have his statue on the University campus, though the teachers opposed it saying Khonangthava was neither a religious leader nor an academician. Mass murders, burning of books, denouncing Indian tradition and laws, nude demonstrations against army 'brutalities' and Delhi's rule and opposing anything that makes Manipur undisputedly a part of the national mosaic are the signs representing this tiny state of the famous Radha Krishna dance forms and a great tradition of literature. Nothing is being done for this barbarous activities which is being committed unabated.

Ladakh: But if a Manipur has to face the brutal indifferences of Delhi and harsher attitude of the gun wielding terrorist groups, the same is true about the northern jewel Ladakh. Forced conversion of Buddhist girls, continuous victimisation of Leh region and people on the basis of their religion, lesser opportunities to the youth for employment and no patient hearing of their demands has been the hallmark of Ladakh affairs since last many years. Ladakh Buddhist Association has been up in arms and fighting a lonely battle all these years with several hundred pages of memorandums sent to Ministry of Home Affairs and other party leaders with no results.

Out of 2,22,236 sq kms of the J&K state, Jammu has 26,293 sq kms and Ladakh 1,38,942 sq kms. It must be remembered that 78,114 sq kms of the state is under illegal occupation of Pakistan, 37,555 sq kms under illegal occupation of China and 5,180 sq kms have been illegally handed over to China by Pakistan. While Ladakh constitutes 69.60 % of the state's total land area, Kashmir valley, the most turbulent and vocal one is just 11.48% and Jammu 18.92%. Within Ladakh Buddhist majority district Leh has 45,110 sq kms and Shia Muslim majority district Kargil has 13,000 sq kms. While Kargil has shown an extraordinary growth in population of 17.34% in the *sic* years between 1981-1991, Leh population grew at the rate of just 9.10%. Even in Leh district the population of Muslims increased from 15.32% in 1981 to 18.37% in 1991 (projected).

Buddhists fear an assault on their culture and traditions through the conversion of Buddhist girls and a planned effort to outnumber Buddhists through a population aggression. In 1992 an agreement was signed between the Ladakh Muslim Association and Ladakh Buddhist Association, the supreme organisation of Ladakh representing Buddhists at the intervention of Ministry of Home Affairs ensuring that the Buddhists converted to Islam shall be allowed to return to their original faith, but the Muslims never honoured the agreement. The following points were... raised by the Buddhist Association in a memorandum to the Central Govternment during NDA rule :

1. During 1992-99 period/24 Buddhist girls from Leh district were converted to Islam and majority of them were taken to Kargil.
2. Twelve villages with hamlets of Buddhists, comprising 651 families (numbering app. 5,000 persons) located at 40kms to 60 kms from Kargil town were targetted for conversions. Till 2002, 72 boys and girls were converted to Islam as per the survey conducted by the Ladakh Buddhist Association.
3. Muslims of Kargil are not allowing the LBA to repair and reconstruct a 40 year old Gompa comprising three rooms and at present lying in shambles.
4. Cremation of dead Buddhists is not allowed at Kargil and the body has to be moved at a remote Buddhist area.

5. No Buddhist Sarai is allowed to be constructed at Kargil though there has been a demand for the last 35 years.
6. Six new mosques have been constructed at Leh town during 1989-99 in close vicinity of Buddhist habitations and in a planned manner more than 540 Muslim families have been settled at Leh, majority of them coming from Kargil.
7. Kargil has 20% Buddhist population. Yet (a) only one Buddhist was appointed as *patwari* out of 24 *patwaris*, the rest were all Muslims. (b) In 1998, 40 employees for class IV were appointed in education department, out of these only one was Buddhist, that too after his conversion to Islam.

Similar complaints, with proven statistics were given regarding discrimination against Buddhists in the area of Kashmir Administrative Services (KAS), admission to medical and engineering colleges, and allocation of development funds received from the Central Government. Needless to say such discriminations fuel the anger and communalise the polity in an ugly manner if proper corrections are not made immediately. It is heartening that after the UPA Government took over, Mufti Md. Sayed's govt. in J & K redressed some of these problems. Yet the demand for a separate Union Territory status to Ladakh has gained momentum and popular leaders like Mr. Thupstan Chhewang have been elected to Lok Sabha by thumping majority under the banner of U.T.Morcha. It is noteworthy that Mr. Thupstan had been a strong Congress leader before. There is one moot point regarding J & K though the Central Government and Indian army have been helping the people of Kashmir valley at the cost of the other states' development, the unrest and anti-Indian feelings in the valley have shown an increase rather than getting subsided. Recently a Hurriyat leader went to Pakistan and expressed his gratefulness to a Pakistani Minister for providing training to about 1,500 Kashmiri Mujahideens. If he is so grateful for such a gesture which would not involve more than a few lakh rupees, what about expressing the same gratefulness to the Indian army which has spent thousands of crores and laid by precious lives of Jawans to defend and develop valley people? Not a single word has come so far about even an idea of such gratefulness. Here is an interesting data regarding Army's ambitious Sadbhavna Operation—to win the hearts of Valley Muslims. But the result is anybody's guess.

Contribution of army to local economy (For year 2000-2001)

Hiring of civilian transport (For army duties)	10.04 crores
Hiring of ponies/porters	9.65 crores
Purchase of cooperative marketing Societies to meet 43% of army requirement	2.5 crores
* Profit to local flourmills	0.35 crores
* Engagement of labour at Army depots	2.8 crore
Total	**35.34 crores***

Note: In addition to this the transportation contracts for which the suppliers are mainly from Srinagar are to the tune of Rs. 2.2 crores per annum.

Students covered under army Goodwill schools:

Leh District	Kargil district
550	700

Note: The army has adopted the District BAL Ashram at Kargil, which houses 47 orphans. Army is also running a boys hostel at Drass.

Girls Covered Under Vocational Training: Approximately 700 girls are being imparted a composite training package in Vocational Training Centres within a schedule of one year which includes various skills like tailoring, knitting, carpet weaving, computer training and a comprehensive education package for enhancement of their qualification.

Adult Education: Army undertook a massive adult education drive to set up one Adult Education centre in each Army unit's area of responsibility thus aiming at educating at least a batch of 3,600 non-literate women between the age of 18 and 35 in a 8 months cycle.

Operation Sadbhavana was projected as a long-term strategy for a speedy assimilation of Jammu and Kashmir into rest of the country.

Community Development: Rural electrification in selective areas was undertaken including the village irrigation and anti-drought schemes. Village cooperatives in poultry farming, vocational training for unemployed youths, resources centres at Leh, Kargil and Dras for mentally and physically challenged, orphanage at Kargil. Boys hostel at Dras, cultural fusion by mass community participation and revival of local culture, traditions, including horse polo and archery was initiated.

So much was the impact that AFP reported, 'nowhere in the world any army has ever done so much of development and social integration work that was done by Jawans in Kashmir'. But some how, Kashmir continues to remain in the clutches of a 20 year old Pakistan supported anti-Indian insurgency that has left 65,000 people dead by the official count. Separatists put the count at between 80,000 and 100,000. [Agency France Press, September 14, 2003]

The extensive details about the army's involvement in social development sector is that this is exactly the area ignored by media rubbishing it as a public relations exercise. It is extremely painful. That army's goodwill gestures failed to bring in the desired results should make us think the real source of the hate and animosity towards the Indian state by Kashmir's Islamists and remedies found accordingly.

A nation is not made of a large amount of forex or infrastructural progress alone. It is the spirit of its people and a unique value system, beliefs and a distinct vision, the cultural and civilisational hue and a will to win in every field one enters, that makes it live and invincible and gives it an honourable place in the comity of nations.

Smaller nations than India have achieved this on their own. This requires a great deal of self-confidence and a deep-rooted sense of patriotism.

Love of the mother land means an uncompromising attitude towards security issues too. No amount of prosperity can provide stability in the absence of a ruthless security preparedness and a will to eliminate the enemies within and without with a single-minded zeal. We certainly have come a long way and one can only hope that political expediency would not obstruct the path of ensuring safe borders and impeccable safety to the patriotic citizens within our boundaries.

10

Deprivation: A Conflict Maximiser

Abnash C. Julka

"There can be no advantage in suppressing an eruption; it must have its vent. If, therefore, before we can remain at peace, we must fight amongst ourselves, it is better that we do so."

– M.K. Gandhi (Hind Swaraj)

"How is India doing?" is a question that continues to engage the attention of the best of Indian minds and India-watchers, the world over. The answer to this question cannot be a simple and straight one. For, India is not just another country on the world-map; it is a world unto itself.

Given her civilizational history, varied patterns of regional settlements, wide topographic, demographic, caste, religion, and linguistic variations, massive population (projected to overtake China in not too distant a future), and an economy billed to be the 'Third Largest', summarising the Indian experience is not easy. Availability of different perspectives and points of reference makes the task even more difficult. It is not therefore, surprising to find phrases like 'India Shining' and 'India Whining' as the polar expressions about the country's development performance.

Our data machines have churned out facts in support of each of these partial truths and partisan frames. Both of these, indeed, are the facets of the Indian reality but neither passes off as "the Indian economic reality" which, like Janus, has two faces, looking in opposite directions.

If we undertake a journey in time and care to examine our development experience against the background of our colonial past,[1] *the brighter side* of India shows up. The first fifty years of Indian Republic saw a nine-fold increase in its Gross Domestic Product (at constant, 1993-94 prices), a trebling of real per capita incomes, doubling of life expectancy at birth, near four-fold literacy rate, and a quadrupling of food-grains output.[2] All those achievements are in the face of a three-fold increase in population, wastage of human and material resources in fighting five wars and a spatially dispersed militancy, and a 'soft-state' with a functioning democracy. On the *flip side,* we are a country which accounts for the largest number of malnourished children in the world. We are home to some half of the planet's hungry people. We are a nation where nearly nine out of ten pregnant women, aged between 15 and 49 years, suffer from malnutrition and anaemia.[3] As if that is not ominous enough, the Economic Survey 2001-2002 informed that some 260 million of us lived below the *'official' poverty line in 1999-2000.*[4] And, for the same year, the number of unemployed stood at 26.58 million. India-Vision 2020 [GOI, 2004, p. 32] cautions, 'Major changes in economic policy and strategy will be needed to eliminate the current (2002) backlog of more than 34 million unemployed job-seekers and assure employment opportunities for all additions to the labour force'.

Thus, the independent India has both a bright side and a dark side to its growth record. A high-growth trajectory stretching over immediate past two decades and the 'Hindu-rate of growth', lasting the first three decades of planned development spelt hope for some and despair for others. While growth there was, the distributive justice was missing. There lay sources of conflict, posing serious threat to our security from within.

II
Of 'Snakes and Ladders' - Interpretting the Indian Experience

In Ludo, a simple game of dice, snakes and ladders are distinct and dispersed entities. Therein, a snake-bite brings a downfall by several notches, a ladder enables a player to move upwards, skipping several slots in the process. The outcome of a game is solely determined by chance according to throw of a dice, dexterity and wisdom of a player has no role. The ludo of real life differs from that simple game in two aspects.[5] Here the snakes and ladders are not distinct, the same opportunity can manifest as a snake or as a ladder depending on the choice one makes and the play of 'chance' or 'destiny'.

We, in independent India, made a pledge. Jawaharlal Nehru,[6] the first Prime Minister of India, addressed the Constituent Assembly on 14-15 August, 1947 in the following words :

Long years ago we made a tryst with destiny, and now the time comes when we shall redeem our pledge, not wholly or in full measure but very substantially. At the stroke of the midnight hour, when the world sleeps, India will awake to life and freedom. A moment comes, which comes but rarely in history, when we step out from the old to the new, when an age ends, and when the soul of a nation, long suppressed, finds utterance............We end today a period of ill-fortune and India discovers herself again.

That discovery meant defining and realising an India 'based on equity and social justice and social and economic equality'. One can notice the idealism and resolve to re-build India as a just society. Our Constitution is an expression of the vision and values of its founding fathers. It manifests the social, political, and economic ethos of the times. It sums up our faith and embodies the aspirations of our people.

Let us recall that the Preamble to the Constitution of our country reads —

We, the People of India, having solemnly resolved to constitute India into a

Sovereign [Socialist and Secular] *Democratic Republic and to secure to all its citizens;

Justice,.	social, economic and political;
Liberty,	of thought, expression, belief, faith and worship;
Equality	of status and of opportunity, and to promote among them all.
Fraternity	assuring the dignity of the individual and the unity [and integrity][7] of the Nation

in our Constituent Assembly do hereby Adopt, Enact, and Give to Ourselves this Constitution. A men!

Mind the words, "We, the People of India"; One people, people of India and no other contextual identities have been alluded to.

Described as 'a pledge to our people and a pact with the civilised world', the Constitution incorporated the Fundamental Rights and included the Directive Principles[8] of state policy in an attempt at creation of an egalitarian society through a non-violent social revolution.

In plain simple terms, it promised Bread + Dignity + Freedom for all. Democracy, with universal adult suffrage, Mixed-Economy model, with increasing emphasis on the public sector, and Federalism, to facilitate the process of nation-making, were chosen to see India home — having set a 'Socialistic pattern of society'. A network of institutions and extensive policy apparatus was created towards that end only.

Things did work under the state-led, import-substituting industrialisation. We experienced nine years (1956 to 1965) of rapid growth, with industry on the fore-front. For once, scarcity regime seemed over; there were jobs, incomes, and goods for the asking. Since the administrative structure and communication & transport systems were further strengthened and expanded, there were jobs in plenty in the administration, public utilities, and the public sector. Planning and regulatory machinery translated into additional cushy jobs and considerable accretion of powers in the hands of politico-administrative authority. More money and more power, without any accountability and transparency in decision-making, also meant greater temptation for exercising discretion. A social system so used to 'traditional authority' with its spirit of grace, class-caste affinity, and personal whims could not rise to the occasion and meet the demands of 'rational-legal authority'.

Idealism gave way to pragmatism. Only a handful, with a strong courage of conviction, could follow the ideals of democracy and the spirit of the constitution. The rest stumbled and subjugated the rational-legal to the traditional hierarchical regime. It was an ominous sign of ladders turning snakes. A 'rent-seeking' and 'corrupt-society' was beginning to emerge.[9] Was it a nation-in-making or the process of un-making a nation? Perhaps the latter was the answer.

It was no longer democratic politics; this was business pure and simple, though under different garbs. As one observer[10] put it :

> 'India is a peculiar democracy, it is the only functional democracy in which political parties have no stable, legitimate, established sources of income.......... It is not supporters (members) who fund parties, it is parties that reward members....Hence, it is important for parties to get into government, and to siphon off government funds .... Politics based on the capture and sale of state power is expensive and unstable.'

Naturally, like business cartels, one heard of the 'Baman-Bania Combine',the 'Muslim-Yadav' force and the 'Dalit-Muslim' power, just to name a few, rather than political parties with a National Vision and Mission. The divisive 'vote-bank' politics transformed the instruments of progression into tools of regression — ladders turning into snakes.

The economy in general, and public sector and public policy in particular, suffered in the process. It was argued by Robert Wode (1991) that, 'If a country is to make the leap to sustained growth, its government must be able to resist the pressures of special interest groups — an authoritarian government is better placed to do this than a democratic one'. There is some merit in the above argument, particularly in the context of up-coming economies and nations in the making. Democracy has to be guided to ensure economic discipline; frugal conduct of the governments is a crime committed against the nation.[11]

Public sector, envisaged to attain commanding heights and serve as the motor force of desirable change, turned into a non-performing resource sucker. In 1989-90, with an approximate reproducible capital stock of over Rs. 3,25,000 crores, it yielded a return of around 1.5 per cent. Rather than generating a surplus for the economy, it needed more and more state support to keep going — once again an example of the ladder turning into a snake.

The private-sector (the India Inc.) was not doing better either in terms of its growth performance; high tariff-walls and regulatory apparatus was in place to ward off competition and protect its inefficiency. A low-quality, high-cost, inegalitarian structure emerged.

Interestingly, the competitive internal politics and the 'Foreign-hand' combined to produce scores of conflicts by espousing various sub-national, religious, ethnic, cultural, caste, linguistic and provincial identities. Scarcity regime was back in place. Parochialism was promoted. 'Sons of the soil' ideology was advocated with fervor. Ignoring the ideal — 'We the people of India', every attempt was made to highlight contextual and sub-national identities for defining 'we' and the 'other' just to corner further economic gains and additional political space. The state chose to buy off the conflicts through extension of reservations for various groups, distribution of doles and evolving a system of subsidies. Fiscal imbalances, excessive borrowing, and frequent bouts of inflation were a natural corollary on the financial front (See Fig. 1). These moves had a socio-political fallout as well; 'kamandal' was pitted against the resurrected 'Mandal' — Vandalism followed, people took to streets.

What was more damaging than the fiscal crisis was that the process of national consolidation was put in the reverse gear. Rather than helping in the process of relegation of sub-national identities and caste prejudices, this form of state-craft not only kept those issues alive but also fueled them. A nation was pitted against itself.

This form of governance (or mis-governance) is a clear illustration of subordinating public policy to suit personal/private interests. This also shows how the opportunities for making India a strong nation, living at peace with itself, were used to the contrary effect by the vested interests. Having conceded 17 demands for separate States and Union Territories, with 5 secessionist and separatist demands, 12 ongoing movements for separate States and Union Territories,[12] and vast pockets of insurgency and terrorism, if India has not dis-integrated, it is not because of those politicians, it is in spite of them. There is still an invisible bond — a tradition, a history, a meta-culture — which is holding us together.

III
Threats to India's Internal Security : What keeps the Pot Boiling ?

A country is as secure as its people are. Secure people are at peace with themselves and social synergy increases in the society. We must understand that, 'The battle of peace has to be fought on two fronts'. The first is the security front where victory spells freedom from fear. The second is the economic and social front where victory means freedom from want. Only victory on both fronts can assure the world of an enduring peace.[13] As a country, India is no exception to this rule. For lasting peace and harmony, it needed to guard both the frontiers well. Barring the 1962 debacle, she could secure its external borders well. However, the same cannot be said about the second front — freedom from want for her people, millions are still deprived and insecure. For most people today, a feeling of insecurity arises more from worries about daily life than from the dread of a cataclysmic world event. Job security, income security, health security, environmental security and security from crime — these are the emerging concerns of human security all over the world, and India shares these concerns. Almost all of these concerns can be addressed to, provided the nation is creating sufficient wealth and there is political will to do so.[14] Plenty, by itself, can in no way take care of everything. All that is being stated is that if (i) there is economic growth, (ii) it is participatory, (iii) it is distributed well, and (iv) there is a welfare state, then the necessary conditions for creating such a secure society stand fulfilled. A ruthless, rootless, jobless, voiceless, and futureless growth[15] is generative of insecurities for the people. It is an invitation to conflicts in the nation and a potent mix for creating social fission.

Such a state of affairs may lead to alienation of individuals and groups, which can easily be exploited by the conflict maximisers, internal as well as external.

The post independence Indian experience fits the bill. We did have economic growth but it was unevenly distributed across time, space, and persons/groups.

We notice that, at the aggregate level, there is deceleration upto 1981 and acceleration thereafter. Further, the tertiary sector growth has been, more or less, steady and invariably faster than that of the total output.

Table - 1

Indian Economy (1951-2001) :
Decadal Growth Rates (% p.a.)

Period *Sector*	*1951-61*	*1961-71*	*1971-81*	*1981-91*	*1991-2001*
Primary	3.08	2.35	1.61	3.71	3.26
Secondary	6.22	5.54	3.97	7.12	5.95
Tertiary	4.16	4.64	4.33	6.52	7.48
Gross Domestic Product	3.91	3.70	3.08	5.46	5.72

Source : Computed from Economic Survey, various years.

A relative decline of the primary sector and an ascent of the tertiary sector is self-evident; it is more or less change of places for the two over this period. It could have been taken as a sign

Table - 2
Indian Economy : Structure of Output
(% share in GDP, 1993-94 prices)

Sector / Average *for the period*	*Primary*	*Secondary*	*Tertiary*
1950-51 to 1952-53	58.5	13.4	28.1
1991-92 to 1992-93	34.4	24.0	41.6
2000-01 to 2002-03	25.6	24.7	49.7

Source : Same as Table -1

of economic maturity, had it been accompanied by a corresponding shift in the occupational structure as well. However, in our case, the distribution of labour force remained highly skewed in favour of the primary sector. On the last count, it was over sixty per cent for the primary sector and some twenty per cent in the tertiary sector. No wonder that the ratio of farmers income to that of others worsened from 1 : 2 (1960-61) to 1 : 6 (1999-2000); the rural urban divide increased. And, in their bid for power, political leaders coined, 'India-Bharat' dichotomy, stretching from the geo-political to the notional, to exploit the situation. Sharad Joshi has been the most articulate of the lot.[16]

"In 1978, some years after I became a practising farmer in the small village of Ambe then in Pune district of Maharashtra, I had put forward the idea of a neo-colonial exploitative relationship between the two notional entities 'India' and 'Bharat'........... I made it clear right at the outset that these were not geographical entities, and had no territorial frontiers...........

'India' is that notional entity, largely Anglicised and relatively better-off, that had obtained the succession of colonial exploitation from the British; while 'Bharat' is largely rural, agricultural, poor and backward that was being subjected to colonial-like exploitation even after the end of the Raj."

While such a formulation enabled the big farmers, with substantial marketable surplus, to consolidate their financial position (on the strength of various subsidies and increasing MSPs), on one hand, it increased their political clout, atleast on the level of States, on the other, their growing political ambitions were manifested through various protests, winning the support of rural masses by playing upon the said dichotomy.

In Punjab, this brand of rural-urban divide, combined with a feeling of being discriminated against, as perceived and articulated by the landed gentry, culminated in a sharp division on communal lines. The army of unemployed educated rural youth got swayed by emotions and a terrible phase of militancy followed. No doubt those exogenous factors (like having a hostile neighbour, surviving on 'hate-India' compaign) were also at play in fanning the trouble and sponsoring that secessionist demand but deprivation — real or perceived — was no mean a contribution the endogenous front.[17]

Poverty, Inequality, and Unemployment are also forms of deprivation. By arousing a sense of exclusion amongst the affected, these can form a fertile breeding-ground for conflict. As mentioned earlier, even if slow to begin with, economic growth did take place in India but it was not distributed well. Consequently, the poverty graph of the country presented a dismal picture for quite some time (See Figure -2). Not that poverty was new to us. It was glorified or fatalistically accepted as part of the natural scheme of things,[18] in the past. In independent India, things had to be different. To quote Bipin Chandra,[19] "The freedom struggle was also a struggle for economic development..... From the initial stage, the movement adopted a pro-poor orientation which was strengthened with the advent of Gandhi and the rise of the leftists who struggled to make the movement adopt a socialistic outlook". Naturally, people expected salvation, atleast freedom from suffocating poverty, at the earliest.

Moreover, poverty was not uniformally distributed over the politico-administrative divisions of the country.

Table-3 shows spatial distribution of poverty in 17 major states. As we can see absolute poverty appears to be concentrated in Assam, Bihar, Madhya Pradesh, Orissa, and Uttar Pradesh.

Table - 3
Income Poverty in India — Dispersion over Time and Space
(1973-74 to 1999-2000)

S. No.	*States*	*Time Period*					
		1973-74	*1977-78*	*1983*	*1987-88*	*1993-94*	*1999-2000*
1.	Andhra Pradesh	48.86	36.31	28.91	25.86	22.19	15.77
2	Assam	51.21	57.15	40.47	36.21	40.86	36.09
3	Bihar	61.91	61.55	62.22	52.13	54.96	42.60
4	Gujarat	48.15	41.23	32.79	31.54	24.21	14.07
5	Haryana	35.36	29.55	21.37	16.64	25.05	8.74
6	Himachal Pradesh	26.39	32.45	16.40	15.45	28.44	7.63
7	Jammu& Kashmir	40.83	38.97	24.24	23.82	25.17	3.48
8	Karnataka	54.47	48.78	38.24	37.53	33.16	20.04
9	Kerala	59.79	52.22	40.22	31.79	25.43	12.72
10	M.P.	61.78	61.78	49.78	43.07	42.52	37.43
11	Maharashtra	53.24	55.88	43.44	40.41	36.86	25.02
12	Orissa	66.18	70.07	65.29	55.58	48.56	47.15
13	Punjab	28.15	19.27	16.18	13.20	11.77	6.16
14	Rajasthan	46.14	37.42	34.46	35.15	27.41	15.28
15	Tamil Nadu	54.94	54.79	51.66	43.39	35.03	21.12
16	Uttar Pradesh	57.07	49.05	47.07	41.46	40.85	31.15
17	West Bengal	63.43	60.52	54.85	44.72	35.66	27.02
18	SD	11.92	13.71	14.93	12.37	10.73	13.29
19	CV	23.62	28.88	38.01	35.77	32.69	60.81
20	All India	54.88	51.32	44.48	38.86	35.97	26.10

Source: a) Economic Survey 2001-2002, and Economic Survey 2002-2003

b) Computed

Note : S.D.= Standard Deviation CV = Coefficient of Variation

As against this high-poverty of the Eastern region, the North-Western States saw much less poverty.

Table - 4
Inter-State Disparities in India (1970-71 to 2000-2001)

State of the Union and Union Territory	*Per Capita NSDP (99-2000) at current prices Rs.*	*Ranking according to PCSDP*			
		1970-71	*1980-81*	*1990-91*	*2000-01*
Andhra Pradesh	15,040	16	15	15	12
Assam	10,080	19	19	20	19
Bihar	4,793	22	22	22	22
Delhi	36,992	1	1	1	2
Goa	44,349	3	2	2	1
Gujarat	18,926	7	7	7	10
Haryana	21,105	5	6	4	5
Himachal Pradesh	18,160	9	10	9	8
Jammu & Kashmir	12,373	10	8	14	15
Karnataka	16,411	13	11	11	11
Kerala	17,709	14	12	13	9
Madhya Pradesh	11,764	15	16	17	17
Maharashtra	22,977	4	5	5	6
Manipur	10,723	20	14	16	18
Orissa	9,486	18	17	21	20
Pondicherry	29,383	6	3	6	3
Punjab	22,797	2	4	3	4
Rajasthan	12,752	11	21	12	16
Tamilnadu	18,367	12	13	8	7
Tripura	13,195	21	18	18	14
Uttar Pradesh	9,065	17	20	19	21
West Bengal	14,817	8	9	10	13
India	15,625				

Ranking : 1 for the highest and 22 for the lowest

It is not only the incidence of poverty that varies across the States of the Indian Union but so also is the level of development. A summary statement of the proceedings is available in Table-4.

Even a cursory glance at the figures brings out the bitter truth — at the geographic level, there are areas of plenty co-existing with regions of poverty and backwardness. There is nothing unexpected about this uneven development. Historical developments in conjunction with ecological, cultural, resources, and political diversity can produce economic diversity.[20] However, the sore point is that in spite of elaborate planning exercises and lofty declarations, the inter-state disparities not only persisted but were allowed to increase.[21] Poverty, economic backwardness and poor quality of life, on the average, appear together. Findings of a recent exercise[22] on these inter-relations are given below :

Table - 5
Inter-Correlation Matrix — Dimensions of Development and Poverty in India (2001)

Indicator	HDI	HPI	POV(1)	PC NSDP	PQLI
HDI Human Development Index: (HDI)	Pearson Correlation Sig. (2-tailed) N=17	-- 	---		
HPI Human Poverty Index:(HPI)	Pearson Correlation Sig. (2-tailed) N=17	 .012	-.60**		
POV(I) Income Poverty: POV (I)	Pearson Correlation Sig. (2-tailed) N=17	 .003	-.67** .101	.41	
PC NSDP Per Capita Net State Domestic Product:(PCNSDP)	Pearson Correlation Sig. (2-tailed) N=17	.74** .001	-.85** .000	-.66** .004	
PQLI Physical Quality of Life Index: (PQLI)	Pearson Correlation Sig (2-tailed) N=17	.95** .000	-.48* .050	-.59*.66** .012	-- .004

Source : Computed

Notes : ** Correlation is significant, at 0.01 level, (2-tailed).

*Correlation is significant, at 0.05 level, (2-tailed)

Sig.(2 -tailed) or p-value= the probability of obtaining results as extreme as the one observed.

If p-value is small (less than 0.05) then the correlation is significant and the two variables are linearly related. If p-value is relatively large (0.50 or more) then the correlation is not significant and the two variables are not linearly related.

N	=	Number of non-missing values
HDI	=	Human Development Index
HPI	=	Human Poverty Index.
POV (I)	=	Income Poverty
PC NSDP	=	Per Capita Net State Domestic Product
PQLI	=	Physical Quality of Life Index

Reading between the lines, the message that one gets is that it is not economic growth, *per se*, that is important in the context of poverty (poverties) but how that growth has been engineered, and distributed that is crucial. Any study of discontent can ill-afford to ignore this material dimension of man's existence. In our case these facts assume added importance because contemporary India has five social blocks — the upper castes, the other backward classes, scheduled castes, scheduled tribes, and religious minorities.[23] These groups, no doubt are variedly dispersed over the length and breadth of this country but they also have their pockets of concentration. Constitutional guarantees, democracy, and competitive-politics of vote-banks ensure that disparities get projected as deprivations experienced by at least one of the latter four groups. Not only that, every attempt is made to point an accusing finger at the centre. Particularly so, if the government there was headed by a different party, centri-fugal forces start operating.

Poverty, in itself, is painful for the unit in its hold, and so is unemployment. However, since the tolerance limits of different units vary, the consequences of prevalence of poverty and unemployment in a society can differ, depending upon the affected age-group and its indoctrination.

For a variety of reasons, educated youth is identified with impatience and volatility. One can only surmise about the outcome if a relatively backward state also has high unemployment amongst the youth (15-29 year age-group). Radicalism, of various shades, is naturally appealing to youth in general and the deprived lot, in particular. Their search for identity, given those objective realities about the distribution of man's worldly goods, may see them taking to adventurism of sorts. Escape from the existing painful conditions can get manifested in deviant behaviour, addictions, crime, protest movements, insurgency, and even terrorism. The following table says it all.[24]

Table - 6
Development and Deprivation :
States of the Indian Union (1999-2000)

State	SDP (per capita) Rank	Reverse Poverty Rank	Reverse Male Youth Unemployment rank	Aggregate Rank
Andhra Pradesh*	09.0	07.0	07.0	23.0
Assam	13.0	13.0	12.0	38.0
Bihar*	16.0	15.0	14.0	45.0
Gujarat	07.0	03.0	01.5	11.5
Haryana	02.0	05.0	01.5	08.5
Himachal Pradesh Pradesh	05.0	02.0	11.0	18.0
Karnataka	08.0	08.0	05.0	21.0
Kerala	06.0	04.0	15.0	25.0
Madhya Pradesh*	12.0	14.0	08.0	34.0
Maharashtra*	03.0	10.0	10.0	23.0
Orissa*	14.0	16.0	16.0	46.0
Punjab	01.0	01.0	04.0	06.0
Rajasthan	11.0	06.0	03.0	20.0
Tamil Nadu	04.0	09.0	09.0	22.0
Uttar Pradesh*	15.0	12.0	06.0	33.0
West Bengal*	10.0	11.0	13.0	34.0

*Naxalite affected States

Sources : Computed

These are only some of the possibilities that have been listed; reality might unfold in numerous other ways, some familiar and predictable others, novel and un-predictable. However, one pattern that emerges from Fig. 3 and Table 6 is : that deprivation, absolute or relative, and geographic-pockets of threat to internal security are linked in no uncertain terms.[25] Seeds of separatism, fundamentalism, subversion, and violent ideology of the left can easily be sown in such a situation, it's an excellent breeding ground for conflict maximisation. Though, in explaining social phenomena, it would be sheer arrogance to claim accuracy and finality, yet the observed link between deprivation and expressions of protest cannot be ignored. Theoretical support and ideological legitimacy for the same exists in Marxism and Maoism. It may, however, be added that engineering conflicts and resorting to violence is not their exclusive preserve. In the post-Naxalbari episode — India (1967), one finds the same radical phraseology being used by all protest movements directed against the state, irrespective of the character of its leadership or the social group involved. The message is clear and loud —Attending to those material deprivations is a necessary condition for tackling threats to internal security of India. An expanding economy, with ample chances for gainful employment and upward mobility, will provide an enabling environment. However, all those efforts can come to a nought if the political process itself remains unreformed. Its distortions need to be corrected at the earliest. Even some of the special provisions existing in the constitution need to be reviewed, (perhaps ! done away with), in the light of our experience. It might sound cynical but if sincerely felt it, *the trio of Legislature, the Executive, and the Judiciary need a thorough overhauling for curing the sickness pervasive in the Indian society.*

Figure - 1 (Wages of Governmental Frugality (1981-82 to 2003-2004

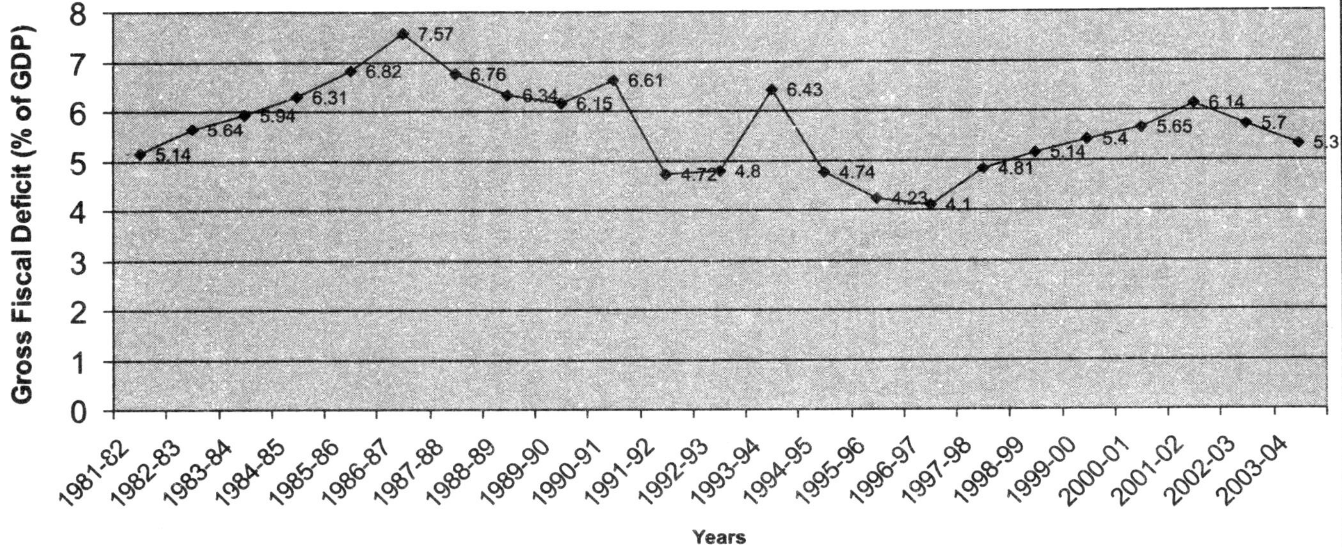

Poverty in India - A Snap Shot of Five Decades
(Percentage of People below the povery line 1951 to 1999-00)

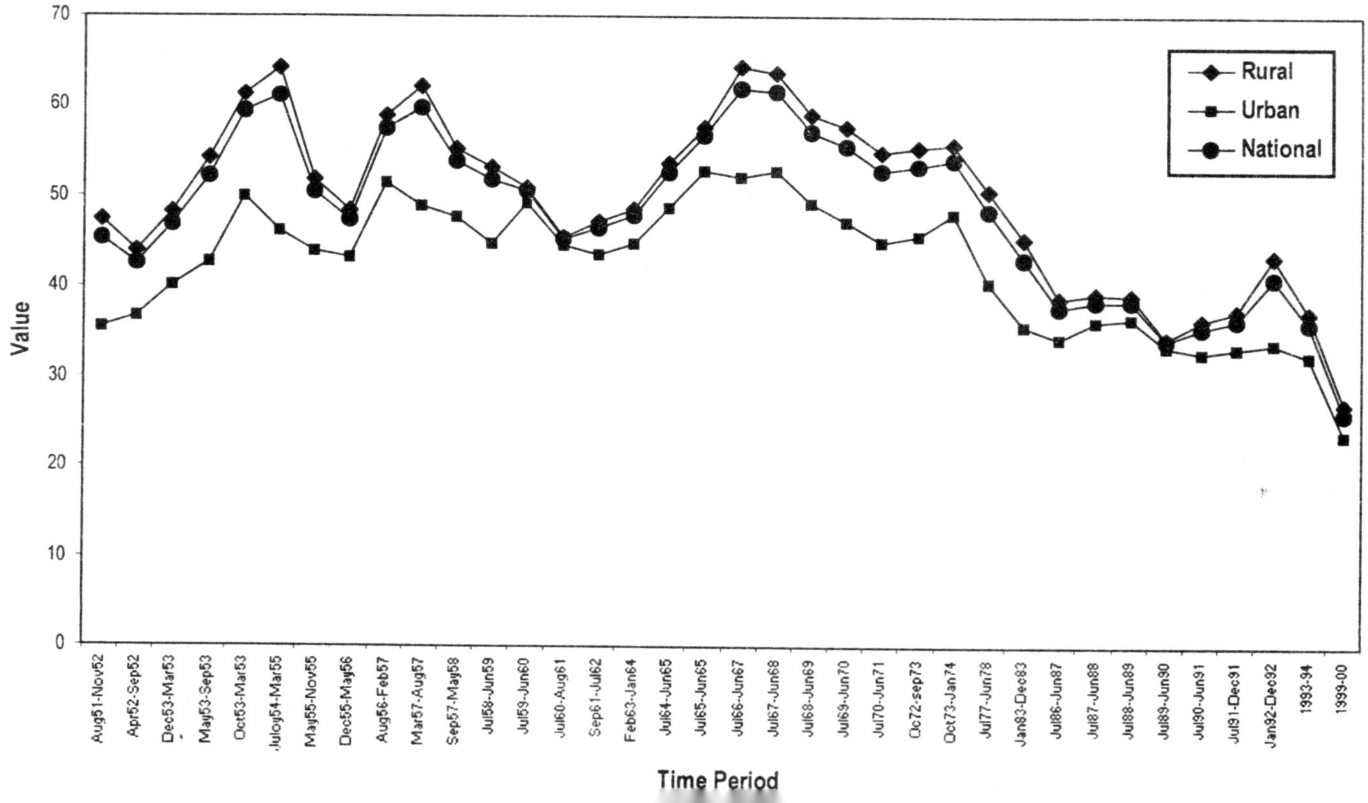

Figure -3

Poverty and Unemployment of Youth : Major States of Indian Union (1999-2000)

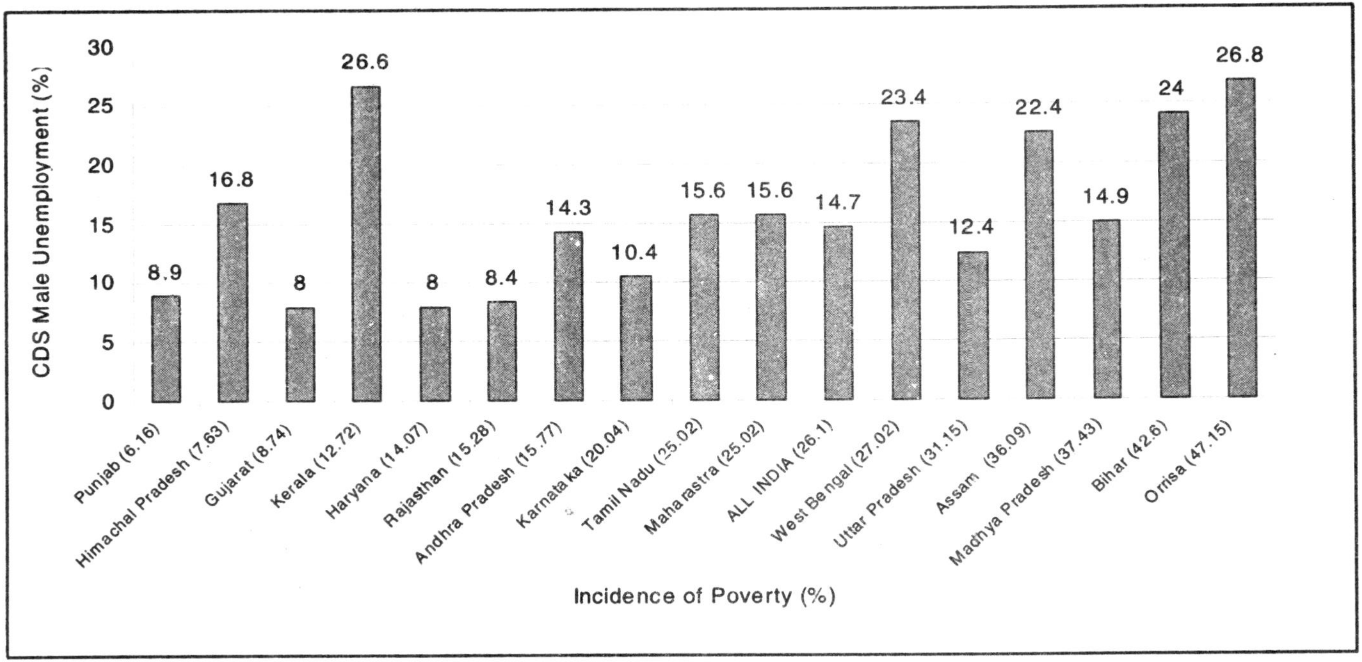

References

1. What was the legacy of the 'raj? — a dilapidated economy, a disrupted society, and a divided territory! India was put on the path of 'guided under-development' [Arun Bose, "Foreign Capital" in V.B. Singh(ed) *Economic History of India 1857-1956,* Allied Publishers Pvt. Ltd., New Delhi, 1965].
2. *Economic Survey, 2003-2004,* Govt. of India, Ministry of Finance, Economic Divison, New Delhi.
3. P.Sainath, "The Poverty of Fiction", *Frontline,* March 12, 2004.
4. These estimates have been faulted with on many a count [See *Economic and Political Weekly,* Vol. XXXVIII, No. 4, January 25-31, 2003;Vol. XXXVIII, No. 14, April 5-11, 2003].
5. The point emerged during an informal chat with Professor Rajesh Kochhar, Director NISTADS, New Delhi.
6. Jawaharlal Nehru, *Speeches,* Vol. 1, p. 25, c.f. Bipan Chandra, et. al. *India After Independence,* Viking, New Delhi, 1999, p. 68; ibid p. 26.
7. Added as per the 42nd Constitution Amendment Act of 1976.
8. To these were added the Fundamental Duties (Part IV A) as per the 42nd Constitution Amendment.
9. One may refer to S.Bhatnagar and S.K. Sharma (eds.) *Corruption in Indian Politics and Bureaucracy,* Ess Ess Publication, New Delhi, 1991, and Chandan Mitra, *A Corrupt Society,* also see Amiya Kumar Bagchi's , "Rent-seeking", *"New Political Economy and Negation of Politics,"* EPW, Aug. 21, 1993, and Arun Kumar's *The Black Economy in India,* Penguin, 2002.
10. Ashok V. Desai, "Fifty Years of India — A Journey in time, *EPW,* Vol. XXXVIII, No. 42, October 18-24, 2003.
11. China, Indonesia, South Korea, Taiwan, Singapore and Hong-Kong [the six fastest growing Asian Countries (1965-1990)]bear testimony to the merits of guided Development/Democracy vis-à-vis economic performance. Even Germany under Bismarck was guided as firmly as Japan under Meiji. The rise to Wealth of most of the big European countries is associated with authoritarian rule.

12. These figures have been taken from T.K. Oommen, *Crisis and Contention in Indian Society*, Sage Publications, New Delhi, 2005.
13. From the US secretary of State's report after the San Franciso Conference (June, 1945), c.f. *HDR* — 1994.
14. *Human Development Report*, 1994, *UNDP*, New York.
15. For explanation of these terms, one may refer to Human Development Report — 1996..
16. *Business Line* (Internet Fdition), February 12, 2003.
17. The movement had its roots in our colonial past. As Chandra (1999) *op.cit.* put it, 'But having unified India, the British set into motion contrary forces. Fearing the unity of the Indian people to which their own rule had contributed, they followed the classic imperial policy of divide and rule....... They succeeded in their endeavours to a varying extent, which laminated in India's Partition'. And, unhesitatingly, we may add that the political leadership in independent India did resort to the same strategy for electoral gains, India kept boiling.
18. Andre Beteille, "Poverty and Inequality", *Economic and Political Weekly*, Vol. XXXVIII.
19. Bipin Chandra, *India's Struggle for Independence*, Viking, New Delhi, 1988.
20. Jawaharlal Nehru in his *The Discovery of India*, Oxford University Press, 1989, (Ninth Impression) made an interesting observation about the close connection between length of British rule and progressive growth of 'poverty' in regions across India.
21. If the coefficient of variation is used as an indicator of disparity then the following trend equation is estimated. CV (Per capita State Domestic Product) = 33.636+0.385 Time, R2 = 0.64 (6.68)
22. Priyanka Julka, Income and Human Poverty in Independent India....., Master's dissertation, P.U., Chandigarh, 2004.
23. See T.K. Oommen, *Crisis and Contention in Indian Society*, Sage Publications, New Delhi, 2005.

For the author, there are six sources of conflict in Indian Society : particularity, inequality, sectorality, peripherality, externality and hierarchy.

24. Joseph Schumpeter, *Imperialism — Social Classes,* Meridian Books, New York, 1955; Robert B. Edgerton, *Deviance: A Cross Cultural Perspective,* Cummings Publishing Co.,London, 1973, Manoranjan Mohanty, *Revolutionary Violence — A Study of the Maoist Movements in India,* Sterling Publishers Pvt. Ltd., New Delhi, 1977; John Kenneth Galbraith, *The Anatomy of Power,* Hamish Hamilton, London, 1983; T.K. Oommen, *Protest and Change,* Sage Publications, New Delhi, 1990, and Maj. Gen. V. Uberoy, *Combating Terroism,* Intellectual Books Corner New Delhi, 1992.

25. Additional empirical support is provided by a strong and positive association between incidence of poverty in a state and that of crime and riots for two points — 1971-73 and 1981-83. The values of Spearman's Rho (σ) range between 0.596 and 0.734 and are statistically significant. Further, it is not just coincidence that almost all the districts 'worst affected' by the problem of insurgency, belong to the list of 150 most backward districts of the country.

11

A Case Study of Bombay Riots and Serial Bomb Blasts in 1992-1993

Amarjit Singh Samra

In the aftermath of demolition of Babri mosque on 6th of December 1992, there were serious communal riots between Hindus and Muslims all over India. These riots took their toll and subsided depending on the intensity of communal feelings and effectiveness of law and order machinery at each place. Two places stood out for a contrast in their handling of security and public safety. The riots went on and on with unprecedented ferocity for two months in the city of Bombay. The mayhem had to be seen to be believed. The city was in flames and streets deserted. Hundreds of people died, thousands were injured and property worth crores was destroyed. The Governor, Chief Minister, Chief Secretary and Police Commissioner were sacked. The contrast was obvious because in the immediate vicinity of Bombay, Thane was peaceful. Thane Commissionerate covers extended suburbs of Bombay, the boundary being a road on one side and bridge on another.

Peace in Thane became a bigger news than riots in Bombay because Thane Police Commissionerate had highly explosive communal pockets like Bhiwandi and Kalyan which had history of riots and returned externess. Interestingly these extended suburbs remained so peaceful that it became a case study for the media and experts. As a result of this, the state of preparedness and police leadership got accolades. The Police Commissioner of Thane was promoted and posted as Police Commissioner of Bombay. Since I happened to be the beneficiary who got credit for maintaining peace, I took charge in Bombay on 30th of January, 1993.

The job was simple. Restore peace and normalcy. The answer was simpler — done, the buck stops here. I took total responsibility. The law of the land will prevail. Laws will be enforced without fear and favour. Law enforcement will be fair and impartial. These were the guiding principles for the law enforcement agency, be it media, politicians and or the public.

This is easier said than done. Fortunately deeds speak louder than words. When I sermonise this in Bombay, it is accepted with some authenticity because of my track record. I have arrested and locked up Ruling party MLA, Opposition MLA, actor son of a ruling party MP, Municipal President of ruling party, councilors, corporators, political heavy weights and busy bodies of all parties under TADA, NSA and other laws. They have been in jails for years maximum being twelve years. Not even in one case there has been an adverse comment from courts, media or politicians. It can happen perhaps only in Maharashtra that I was appointed Police Commissioner by Congress and DGP by BJP-Shiv Sena parties.

Thanks to media, I had come to Bombay with larger than life image. "Samra's foresight kept peace in Thane" said *Times of India*. Others did not lag behind. There was a stampede of over fifty photographers to greet me when I entered the majestic staircase of Police Commissioner's Office. There were showers of adjectives and write-ups from the media :

> The common man's "Super-Cop" (*Indian Express*), 'A Cop That Cheers" (*Times of India*), "Clear headed" (*India Today*), "Samra shows the way" (*Pioneer*), "Bombay's Saviour" (*Hindustan Times*).

I sat down to find out what had gone wrong in Bombay to make it so insecure. Political interference, loud speakers for Izaans, Namaz and Maha-Aarties, lack of preparedness in Police, confusion about the role of Army, public demoralisation, media criticism, communal tension, underworld, serious crimes and so on. These are tough issues, but have been handled in the past by successful leaders. The month of February was spent in addressing these problems and communal harmony programmes. I was happy that we had turned the corner and recovery was fast. By the end of the month, Bombay was normal and police image had hit new heights.

The Bomb Blasts of March, 1993

Barely had we recovered, when we were in for a shock on 12th of March, 1993. Serial bomb blasts took place at twelve places within two hours on a black Friday afternoon. Hundreds of people died and thousands were injured. This was a real test to restore normalcy and communal harmony. We were on the job. Communal Riots Scheme was put into operation. I visited troubled spots and went on local T.V. live to assure the public that give me a little time and I shall get the culprits before them for trial in the court for deterrent action under TADA. I appealed to them to have faith in us and not to contribute to rumours, fear and panic which helped terrorism. The public response was phenomenal which confirmed their confidence in police credibility. The assurances were backed by action.

Within six months, the case was detected, accused was arrested and produced in court for trial. Law enforcement was professional, fair and impartial, without fear or favour. Kudos to police professionalism and work ethics in Bombay. Never has such a complex conspiracy and low cost war been resolved with such speed and authenticity. Media briefings, public response, coordination of Administration, politicians and criminal justice system were nearly perfect. In that process I became a celebrity to earn second promotion within one year to a cooler place as chief of Anti Corruption Bureau. Some called it kicking up. Be that it may. The city of Bombay has become a peaceful place. There is tremendous sense of security and public confidence.

Police, administration and politicians have learnt their lessons. The ever-looming greed of corruption of a metro is a tough challenge, but the public and courts know how to deal with it.

The Effective Answers to the Three Questions : India and its cities are as secure as its public response. Destabilising factors are many and any one can take precedence over the other in a given situation. It can be communal tension at one time, bomb blasts at another. Terrorist's strike, police or Army atrocity, Recruitment crisis, border dispute, water sharing, court judgement, desecration of a statue, corruption, any local issue can create a 'divide'. The list is endless. It goes as far as the fertile imagination of mischief-mongers.

To combat these, those responsible for internal security have to be one step ahead of the mischief mongers. The selection of leaders, their track record and security of tenure are the key. This has to be backed by financial support, regular professional training programmes and on the job state of preparedness. The selectors of police leaders must have the inclination and expertise to assess their ability to engineer an agreement in conflict situations.

> *Experience, professional expertise and capability for timely identification of critical social groups in society should get higher consideration for senior appointments. Positive attitude, concern for human beings, and orientation towards communal harmony will be an added advantage.*

In short, law enforcement needs to be taken seriously. Maintenance of peace and control of crimes are crucial for growth in a civilized society. We recruit the best possible talent for leadership in law enforcement. We have to create laws and a system of justice for them to function effectively and make this country a secure place for its citizens.

12

Bangladesh — A Failed State and Rise of Militant Islam

Baljit Rai , IPS (Retd.)

As no one can choose one's parents, no country can choose its neighbours either. In this matter, India cannot be blamed squarely for having Bangladesh as her neighbour in the East. India has midwifed the birth of Bangladesh in 1971 and brought her freedom from highly exploitative and colonial rule of West Pakistan.

But before we go into details of what has gone wrong in Bangladesh since the assassination of Sheikh Mujib-ur-Rahman, the first Prime Minister and then President of Bangladesh on 15 August, 1975 we must acquaint ourselves with some basic facts. Two of the most important aspects of the nation of Bangladesh, barely 36 years old in its present incarnation, are its gargantuan demography and rise of militant Islam. Regarding the first, the reader may have a careful look at the figures given in the following tables:

Table - I
Bangladesh compared with some of the larger states of India

Name of the country/Indian State	*Area (in sq.km.)*	*Population (in millions)*	*Density (per sq.km.)*
Bangladesh	144000	143.8	1000
Gujarat	196024	50.6	258
Karnataka	191791	52.8	275
Madhya Pradesh	308144	60.3	314
Rajasthan	342299	56.4	165
Uttar Pradesh	238566	166	689
Andhra Pradesh	275069	76	275

It may be noted that even when compared with the large size states of India, Bangladesh is much more densely populated. Its density of population is 2 to 4 times that of the above mentioned states. Another aspect of the population of Bangladesh is poor rate of literacy which is 38% only with female literacy being as low as 13 to 14%. With such massive illiteracy among women one can imagine why population in Bangladesh is exploding.

Table - II
Camparison with seven states in the North-East of India

Name of the country/Indian State	*Area (in sq.km.)*	*Population (in millions)*	*Density (per sq.km.)*
Bangladesh	144000	143.8	1000
Assam	78438	26.6	340
Arunachal Pradesh	837431	1.9	13
Meghalaya	22429	2.3	103
Nagaland	16579	2	120
Manipur	22327	2.3	107
Mizoram	21081	.89	42
Tripura	10486	3.1	304
Total of Indian states	252083	38.4	147 (average)

A close scrutiny of the figures in the above table will show that Bangladesh, although smaller in area than the total area of the above mentioned seven states in the North-east is much more crowded and populous. This entire area has always appeared to the East Bengalis/East Pakistanis/Bangladeshi as almost vacant land and enough to accommodate the rapidly expanding population of Bangladesh. It was for no other reason that Zulfiqar Ali Bhutto had said, "Our controversy with India is not on the problem of Kashmir only. In Assam there are some Muslim majority districts which should have been given to Pakistan at the time of the Partition. These districts were wrongly given to India." (*Myth of Independence* by Z.A.Bhutto, OUP, Karachi, 1969).

Bhutto's assertion is totally baseless. The fact is that Assam had no Muslim majority district except Sylhet which was given to Pakistan.

Similarly Sheikh Mujib-ur-Rehman, that spurious icon of secularism, had thus expressed himself, "The population of East Bengal is increasing at alarming speed. The inhabitants face acute shortage of land. The Bengalis need land which can be given by Assam. Assam abounds in good forests and beautiful scenes of nature. If some inhabitants of Bangladesh migrate to Assam and settle there permanently, they will be very happy. Actually Assam should have been included in East Pakistan". (*Eastern Pakistan: Its Population and Economie, Pakistan Renaissance Society, Calcutta*). This attitude and brazenness is the key to the understanding of the acute problem of illegal till date and never-ending infiltration of Bangladeshi Muslims into India.

It seems that the views expressed by Sheikh Mujib-ur-Rehman have become the cornerstone of the policy and the grand design of expanding present day Bangladesh into Greater Islamic Bangladesh. Another important aspect that seems to have escaped the notice of secularists in this country is the near total ethnic cleansing of Hindus in Bangladesh whose lands and property were forcibly occupied by Muslims without paying compensation or paying nominal compensation. Thus the Bangladeshi Muslims first terrorised and drove out Hindus from Bangladesh and then illegally infilterated into India in search of 'living space'. Thus Hindus have been losers in Bangladesh and they are losers in India as well! These are the wages of bogus and cowardly secularism being practised by political parties in India. One disastrous effect of this policy has been that population of Hindus in Bangladesh instead of increasing has been reduced from 30% in 1947 to less than 10% today. What happened to the Nehru -Liaquat Pact of 1950 which was designed to provide security to minorities in India and Pakistan ? While Muslims prospered by leaps and bounds in India, Hindus and Hinduism disappeared in Pakistan and Bangladesh.

Media Reports on Infiltration of Bangladeshi Muslims

Indian media have always been in the forefront in highlighting the problem of infiltration from Bangladesh but who cares. Below are given just a few headlines out of a pletheora of such reports appearing in various newspapers over the years.

1. "Serious influx from Bangladesh— *Statesman*, 6.4.1990.
2. "Bangladesh refugees demand Indian citizenship— *Statesman*, 13.2.1991.
3. "Bangla influx could upset India's demography— *Statesman*, 1.11.1992.
4. "Population boom via infiltration— *Statesman*, 13.4.1992.
5. "Muslim Banga Bhoomi sought— *Statesman*, 23.9.1992.
6. Deportation may erode left base—*Statesman*, 20.10.1992.
7. "Editorial" Push, Pull and Eject"— *Statesman*, 23.9.1992.
8. "The unending refugee inflow— *The Weekend Observer*, 3.10.1992.
9. "Delhi alone has three lakh Bangla nationals"— *Hindustan Times* - 31.5.1992.
10. "Silent Threat to Integrity"— *The Tribune*, 9.11.1992.
11. Dangerous influx: Another partition in the offing—*The Week*, 12.7.98.

12. Influx of Bangladeshis (Read Muslims) swell Naga population— *Hindustan Times,* 22.8.98.
13. Unauthorised Bangladeshis may upset pollmath—*The Tribune,* 23.7.99.
14. Annexation of Assam is latest ISI interest— *Indian Express,* 22.8.99.
15. ISI Plan to carve out new country (comprising border districts of West Bengal, Assam and Bangladesh from their parent State and set up new Islamic country)— The *Tribune,* 14.12.99.
16. Bangladeshi immigrants a threat to NE's security: Experts—*Nation,* 12.1.2000.
17. Alarming Influx, Bangladesh and Comrade Inderjit Gupta: An editorial under the caption "Alarming Influx"— The *Tribune,* 8.5.97.

The Indian media cried hoarse but it did not produce the slightest ripple in the ruling elite in Congress party.

Internal Situation in Bangladesh — Rise of Militant Islam

In a recent study by Foreign Policy journal of the Carnegie Endowment for International Peace and Fund for Peace, Bangladesh has been held to be as one of sixty countries in the world which are all failed states. Unfortunately, India is surrounded by failed states on all sides. The failed states index ranks countries on 12 economic, social and political parameters which are as under:

(i) Demographic pressures

(ii) Refugees and displaced persons

(iii) Group grievances

(iv) Human flight

(v) Uneven development

(vi) Economic decline

(vii) Delegitimisation of state

(viii) Public services

(ix) Human rights

(x) Security apparatus

(xi) Factionalised elites, and

(xii) External intervention.

The failing states are a threat to world peace and today USA feels threatened less by conquering states than failing ones. The same is true of India. Failed states export undesirable and deadly things such as international terrorists, large scale immigrants, drugs, weapons etc. Bangladesh, which has sunk into Islamic fundamentalism is guilty on all these counts and is deliberately complicating things for India particularly in the fragile polity of North-eastern states.

Bomb Explosion of August 2005

17th August, 2005 will always be remembered as the day on which more than 500 bombs exploded almost simultaneously within half an hour in 63 of the 64 districts of Bangladesh. On this day Bangladesh revealed to the world its potential for Islamic terrorism. The country which would be most affected by these developments is India. Internal chaos in Bangladesh can push millions of people into India as happened in 1970-71 thereby creating unprecedented social, political and economic upheaval.

Islamic Organisation

Pakistan has never been able to digest the secession of East Pakistan in 1971 and her one endeavour ever since has been to somehow bring Bangladesh back into its orbit, both politically as well as its Islamic adjunct. Pakistan has been eminently successful in not only eliminating Shiekh Mujib-ur-Rehman and his entire family but also accelerating the process of Islamisation of Bangladesh. Some of its acheivements are removal of the state principle of secularism from the Constitution in 1977 and declaration of Islam as the state religion in 1988. Friday replaced Sunday as a weekly holiday. But the major change and achievement was the centre stage and space that came to be reoccupied by fundamentalist organisations like Jamate-Islami which had supported Pakistan against its own freedom fighters in the Civil war in 1970-71. It is now again so powerful and influential that it is a part of the ruling coalition headed by BNP (Bangladesh National Party). Other Islamic Organisations operating in Bangladesh are :

I. Islami Oikyo Jote (an alliance of Seven militant Islamic groups)

II. Islamic Chhatra Shibir (ICS) — Jamata's Student body founded in 1977, maintains close links with the SIMI (Student Islamic Movement of India) now banned by the Government of India.

III. Harkat-ul-Jihad-al-Islami (HUJI -BD)

All these parties are ardent advocates of *Jihad* and aim at establishing the hegemony of Islam. They are lavishly funded by Saudi Arabia and Pakistan. HUJI-BD was declared a terrorist organisation by USA in 2003.

IV. Jamiat-ul-Mujahideen Bangladesh (JUM-BD) a terrorist organization totally committed to *Jihad.* It advocates *Jihad* against India and all non-Muslims living in Bangladesh. It also runs 39 Madrassas institutions instilling hatred into the minds of the young students.

V. Shahadat-e-al-Hikma (SAH) follow the ideology of of Lashkar-e-Toiba and maintain close links with the Maoists in Nepal.

One of the institutions, which is having most pernicious influence all around are the Madrassas whose number is estimated to be 64,000. Most of these follow Deobandi Islam (extremist Islam — an Indian product) which gave birth to Taliban Movement in Pakistan with horrendous consequences for Afghanistan. The emphasis in teaching in these Madrassas is on teaching Urdu, Persian and Arabic. The students, passing out from these Madrassas are poorly equipped to enter mainstream life and professions. They are easily lured by motivated quarters who capitalise on religious sentiments to create fanatics, rather than Modern Muslims (Salaluddin Babar — a Bangladeshi journalist)

These Madrassas are the power houses of Islam which generate hatred against Hindus and India.

The plight of the secular forces in Bangladesh, if there are any, is pitiable as they are in no position to take on the extremist Islamic ideologies. Any criticism of Islamic parties is at once twisted into criticism and denunciation of Islam which can have dire consequences. Furthermore, Islamic forces are very clear in their mind and categorically assert that democracy as a system of Government does not suit Muslims who must have an Islamic system of government or Nizam-e-Mustafa. One can imagine consequences for India where millions of such fanatics have infiltrated and settled in large pockets. They are the Islamic tinderbox that has the potential to incinerate the democratic way of life in this country.

Other Islamic organisation which is a great mobilizer of Muslims is the World Tableegh Jamaat (propagation of Islam and Conversion) called Bishwa Ijtema. Its annual sessions are attended by a congregation of atleast 40 lac Muslims from all over the world and is known to be the second largest congregation of Muslims in the world. Such is the dismal profile of theocratic Bangladesh.

Rule of Law has virtually disappeared from Bangladesh. In Aug. 2004 there was an attempt on the life of Shekh Hasina Wajid, former Prime Minister. The grenades hurled at her meeting, killed 20 people. No arrest has been made so far. It is suspected that this attempted assassination was inspired by the party in power, the BNP.

A notorious cleric known as Bangla Bhai (his real name was claimed to be Aziz-ur-Rahman and later Siddiqul Islam) forces Muslims to grow beards, say namaz five times a day and compel women to put on veil. He and his organisation is extremely violent and while enforcing Islamic laws have executed scores of people for committing various sins. Bangladesh waded through rivers of blood in 1971, when three million people were killed in nine months. That violence which was unleashed by the assassination of Shaikh Mujib was followed by coups, assassinations and incarceration not only continue unabated but was further directed towards India.

This unfortunate land has not seen peace ever since. Thuggee and assassinations are a consistent features of life in Bangladesh. Last year (2004) three journalists were killed for reporting on corruption and rise of militant Islam. "In Bangladesh Islam is becoming a legitimising political discourse. Once you don that religious mantle who can criticize you! We see this in Pakistan as well, where very few people are brave enough to take on the Islamists. Now this is happening in Bangladesh. The region has become a haven where *Jihadis* can move easily and have access to a friendly infrastructure that allows them to regroup and train. (C. Christine Fair) Quoted in an article, "The Next Islamist Revolution" by Eeiza Griswold, published in Society-March, 2005.

Situation in West Bengal and Bihar

Here is the voice of total despair. Buddhadeb Bhattacharjee, Chief Minister of West Bengal says, "There is a serious problem with some of our neighbours. Bangladesh says that there are no Bangladeshis in India whereas the entire demography of certain parts of the country and West Bengal is being changed due to infiltration. In many places, there are more Bangladeshi settlers than Indians," he said, inaugurating a BSF seminar.

According to Bhattacharjee, there are three kinds of people who come across the border illegally from Bangladesh. "There are groups who spread the message of Islamic fundamentalism and campaign for Muslim rights in Kashmir. Other groups are directly involved In subversive activities. The third group is that of KLO (Kamtapur Liberation Organisation) militants who have sought shelter in Bangladesh after being driven out of Bhutan. All these groups are receiving support from the Bangladesh Government. We can't compromise on this.

The Chief minister said he had tried to take up the matter with Bangladesh home ministry officials. "When I told them of a senior KLO leader who had sought sanctuary in Bangladesh, they denied the fact. It is strange. I have the telephone number and addresses of the KLO leader but Bangladeshi officials are denying it. Though we were talking in Bengali, it seems we failed to communicate with each other," Bhattacharjee added.

For a start, the calculation validated what had hitherto been a conjecture — the population explosion in the border districts of Bengal was giving them a greater say in state politics." (*Times of India,* 24-6-2005)

Is there any voice more authentic than that of the Chief Minister of West Bengal to castigate Bangladesh for pushing Bangladesh Muslims into India. Although there is no mention of the community, yet a reference to changing demographic character of the border districts makes it clear that the infiltrators are Muslims. The following Tables III IV, V and VI clearly support the views of the Chief Minister of West Bengal.

Table - III
Percentage growth of population between 1991 and 2001 in the border districts of West Bengal

	Muslim	*Non-Muslims*	*%age point gain of Muslims*
South 24 Parganas	34.2	11.5	+22.7
North 24 Parganas	23.8	22.6	+ 1.2
Nadia	21.9	18.8	+ 3.1
Murshidabad	28.4	16.4	+12
Maldah	30.7	19.4	+11.3
Kolkata	19.0	0.7	+18.3
South Dinajpur	79.5	41.9	+37.6
Jalpaiguri	31.3	20.4	+10.9
Cooch Behar	18.5	12.8	+ 5.7
Total: West Bengal	25.9	15.3	+10.6

It may be noted that Muslim population in the nine border districts of West Bengal and four districts of Bihar (see table V) the growth of Muslim populations is far in excess of non-Muslims. Kolkata's figures are really frightening. Here Muslim population grew by 19% as against 0.7 of Non-muslims and Muslim %age rose from 17.7 in 1991 to 2(.3 in 2001.

Table - IV
Muslims as a percentage of total population in border districts of West Bengal

	1991	*2001*
South 24 Parganas	29.9	33.2
North 24 Parganas	24.2	24.2
Nadia	24.9	25.4
Murshidabad	61.4	63.7
Maldah	47.5	49.7
Kolkata	17.7	20.3
South Dinajpur	33.0	38.4
Jalpaiguri	10.0	10.8
Cooch Behar	23.4	24.2
Total: West Bengal	23.6	25.2

Percentage of Muslim Population has gone up in every border districts during the decade 1991-2001.

Table - V
Percentage growth of population between 1991 and 2001 in four districts of Bihar

	Muslims	*Non-Muslims*	*Difference*
Kishanganj	35.2	25.0	10.2
Araria	36.1	32.4	3.7
Purnea	44.1	30.8	13.3
Katihar	39.7	25.4	14.3

Table - VI
Muslims as a percentage of population of four districts in Bihar

	1991	*2001*
Kishanganj	65.8	67.6
Araria	40.5	41.2
Purnea	34.5	36.7
Katihar	39.9	42.5

With commendable foresight, T.V. Rajeshwar, former Governor of West Bengal and now Governor of U.P. wrote in mid-nineties of the last century. "Muslims in India accounted for 9.9 per cent in 1951, 10.8 per cent in 1971 and 11.3 per cent in 1981, and presumably about 12.1 per cent in 1991. The present population ratio of Muslims is calculated to be 28 per cent in Assam and 25 per cent in West Bengal accounted for 56 per cent in South and North Parganas, 48 per cent in Nadia, 52 per cent in Murshidabad, 54 per cent in Malda and about 60 per cent in Islampur sub-division of West Dinajpur. A study of the border belt of West Bengal yields some telling statistics: 20-40 per cent villages in the border districts are said to be predominantly Muslim. There are indications that the concentration of the minority community, including the Bangladesh immigrants, in the villages has resulted in the majority community moving to urban centres. Several towns in the border districts are now predominantly inhabited by the majority community but surrounded by villages mostly dominated by the minority community".

Figures have been given showing the concentration of Muslim population in the districts of West Bengal bordering Bangladesh starting from 24 Parganas and going up to Islampur of West Dinajpur district and their population being well over 50 per cent of the population. The Kishanganj district which was part of Purnea district earlier, which is contiguous to the West Bengal area, also has a majority of Muslim population. The total population of the districts of South and North 24 Parganas, Murshidabad, Nadia, Malda and West Dinajpur adds up to 27,337,362. If we add the population of Kishanganj district of Bihar of 986, 672, the total comes to 28,324, 034. (All figures are based on the 1991 Census.) This mass of land with a population of nearly 2.8 crores has a Muslim majority. The total population of West Bengal in 1991 was 67.90 million and of these, 28.32 million are concentrated in the border districts, with about 16-17 million population of minority community being concentrated in this area. This crucial tract of land in West Bengal and Bihar, lying along the Ganges/Hoogly and west Bengladesh with population of over 28 million, with Muslims constituting a majority, should give cause for anxiety for any thinking Indian.

Let us look at the map of Eastern India — starting from the North 24 Parganas district, proceeding through Nadia, Murshidabad, Malda and West Dinajpur before entering the narrow neck of land lying through Raiganj and Dalkola of Islampur sub-division before passing through the Kishanganj district of East Bihar to enter Siliguri. Proceed still further and take a look at the north Bengal districts of Darjeeling, Siliguri. Proceed further and take a look at the north Bengal districts of Darjeeling, Jalpaiguri and Cooch Behar before entering Assam, and its districts of Dhubri, Goalpara, Bonagigaon, Kokrajhar and Barpeta. A more sensitive region in Asia is difficult to locate... The demographic situation today (Year 2005) is far more serious and the advantage is going entirely to Bangladesh and Bangladeshi infiltrators, Who is responsible for this catastrophe will be dealt with a little later.

Situation in Assam

Addressing the Governors' Conference held on 11-12 January, 2003, Lt. Gen. S.K. Sinha (Retd.). Governor of Assam said that, Muslim population of Assam has shown a rise of 77.42 per cent in 1991 from what it was in 1971. The Hindu population has risen by nearly 41.89 per cent in the same period.

Muslim population [as a percentage of total population in Assam] has risen from 24.68 per cent in 1951 to 28.42 per cent in 1991. As per the 1991 Census, four districts (Dhubri, Goalpara, Barpeta and Hailakandi) have become Muslim majority districts. Two more districts (Nawgaon and Karimganj) should have become so by 1998 and one more district (Moregaon) is fast approaching this position.

The growth of Muslim population has been emphasised in the previous paragraph to indicate the extent of illegal migration from Bangladesh to Assam because .... The illegal migrants coming into India after 1971 have been almost exclusively Muslims.

The influx of illegal migrants from Bangladesh into Assam continues unabated. The IM (DT) Act (fortunately now repealed by the Supreme Court) virtually makes the Police helpless in detecting and deporting them. Border fencing commenced in Assam in 1992 and has not yet been completed. It is likely to be completed by 2007. At long last, work on identity cards is also set to commence soon.

We need to take suitable measures to combat the influx of illegal migrants. It is estimated that approximately 4 million illegal migrants have infiltrated into Assam. This influx may be due primarily to economic reason but it poses a grave threat to the demography of Assam. It is also a serious threat to our national security in the light of the longstanding demand for more "living space" in Bangladesh and reports of entrenchment of Al Qaeda and other fundamentalist activities in that country. .... This silent and invidious demographic invasion of Assam may result in the loss of geostrategically vital districts of Lower Assam. The influx of these illegal migrants is turning these districts into a Muslim majority region. It will then only be a matter of time when a demand for their merger with Bangladesh may be made. The rapid growth of Islamic fundamentalism may provide the driving force for this demand. In this context it is pertinent that Bangladesh has long discarded secularism and has chosen to become an Islamic State. Loss of Lower Assam will sever the entire land mass of the North East from the rest of India. A close scrutiny of the following tables VII to IX would reveal the gravity of the situation.

Table - VII
Percentage growth of population between 1991 and 2001 in six districts of Assam bordering Bangladesh

	Muslims	*Non-Muslims*	*Total*
Dhubri	29.5	7.1	22.9
Barpeta	25.8	10.0	18.9
Goalpara	31.7	14.4	23.0
Hailakandi	27.2	13.3	20.9
Karimganj	29.4	14.5	21.9
Cachar	24.6	16.0	18.9

Table - VIII
Percentage growth of population between 1991 and 2001 in three districts of Assam

	Muslims	*Non-* Muslims	*Muslim* population *higher by*	
Naogaon	32.1	11.3	20.8	%age points
Marigaon	27.2	16.3	10.9	-do--
Darrang	28.9	9.6	19.3	-do--

Situation as viewed by the Intelligent Bureau, Govt. of India. Some excerpts from the note circulated in a conference of Director's General of Police held in 2003.

Table - IX
Muslims as a percentage of total population in districts of Assam

	1991	*2001*
Districts bordering Bangladesh		
Dhubri	70.4	74.3
Barpeta	56.1	59.4
Goalpara	50.2	53.6
Hailakandi	54.8	57.6
Karimganj	49.2	52.3
Cachar	34.5	36.1
Three other districts		
Naogaon	47.2	51.0
Marigaon	46.0	47.6
Darrang	32.0	35.6
Total Assam	28.4	30.9

"There has been an accretion to India's security threats from Bangladesh, particularly after the formation of the BNP led government there in October 2001. The points of concern include:

i. Shelter and training to Indian Insurgent Groups (IIGs) and use of BD soil for carrying out action in our border States;

ii. Acquisition of arms by IIGs in Bangladesh and their transportation for use in India;

iii. Growth of radical Islamic groups as also private madrassas spewing hatred against India;

iv. Enlargement of ISI activities with increasing use of Bangladesh soil for espionage in India as also terrorist actions by radical Islamic groups;

v. Efforts to subvert sections in India's border States with indoctrination and training being provided to such elements;

vi. Continuing inflow of illegal migrants resulting in demographic distortions and growing political clout of such illegal migrants in some border States."

The 4,096 kms, long and porous Indo-Bangladesh border makes for easy crossing. The problem of continued unabated influx of large-scale (over 15 million) illegal Bangladeshi migrants into India has assumed serious security implications. Illegal BD migrants, driven by economic forces, have settled in various States including West Bengal (79 lakhs), Assam (50 lakhs), Bihar (4.75 lakhs in the north-eastern districts including Katihar, Sahebganj, Kishanganj and Purnia), Tripura (3.75 lakhs) and Delhi (3.7 lakhs), in Nagaland, the population of Muslims, mostly illegal migrants from Bangladesh, has more than trebled in the last decade — the figure rising from 20,000 in 1991 to over 75,000. Similarly, in Mizoram also, there has been a growth in numbers of illegal Bangladeshi migrants though firm estimates are not yet available.

The illegal BD migrants have significantly altered the demographic complexion particularly of the border districts of West Bengal and Assam. In Assam, the illegal migrants are able to affect State politics in a major way with their having acquired a critical say in around 50 of the 126 Assembly constituencies in the State. ....

.............Cox's Bazar is the main reception point for foreign arms where after these are transported to India through land routes in Bangladesh. ....

..........Bangladesh, particularly Dhaka, has been used as a staging point for sending members of both IIGs and *jihadi groups* to Pakistan and Afghanistan as also for their infiltration into India for action. Several batches of ULFA cadres were flown to Pakistan from Dhaka for imparting training, which was arranged by ISI..................

...........Meanwhile, within Bangladesh there has been a steady growth of the Wahhabi brand of Islam, which encourages 'jihadi' terrorism. The 'Qaumi' madrassas of Bangladesh (estimated to be 90% of total one lakh are the Madrassas which are outside the ambit of Government control)— main purveyors of its doctrines with India-baiting remaining a lynchpin of their teachings. The financial aid to these madrassas comes through charities mainly from Pakistan and Saudi Arabia. The madrassas are used for indoctrination of youth from both sides of the border, as also shelter/transit point by military/suspected Pak ISI operatives, as also as training centers by fundamentalist outfits like HUJAI, JEI, ICS, IOJ, and for infiltration into India.

...........A section of Bangladeshi opinion-makers have already been talking of a Bangladeshi lebensraum in our North East. ....

....................The new document — Pakistan's Alternative Proxy War Base — was finalised in February 2005. It set out how Pakistan had launched a new operation to redouble its destabilising work in India through Bangladesh. It stated that Pakistan was developing Bangladesh as the new base for its anti-India operations, and that it had already shifted almost 200 terrorist training camps from Pakistan Occupied Kashmir to Bangladesh. The document listed several reasons for the shift to Bangladesh. Among these were the following:

1. The India-Bangladesh border is geographically porous and difficult to keep under close surveillance due to its riverine configurations in the West and hilly terrain in the North-East and East.

2. The fencing remains incomplete — out of the total length of 3,287 kilometers sanctioned for fencing, only 1,502 kilometers have been fenced so far. And the fence is of the most elementary kind.

3. Bangladesh's border configuration rests along vulnerable Indian states such as West Bengal, Assam, Meghalaya, Tripura and Mizoram.
4. Bangladesh territory provides ISI with multiple ingress routes to these sensitive states.
5. Bangladesh territory sits astride India's strategic "Siliguri Corridor", India's slender Communication link with its seven North-eastern states. It is easy to play havoc in the Corridor through Bangladesh.
6. The borders of Nepal and Bhutan states that enjoy close links with India as non-Islamic states of South Asia, are within close reach of Bangladesh territory. Pakistan already has established extensive links in these countries.
7. In the belt running parallel to the borders with Bangladesh and significantly deep into Indian territory, reside large sections of illegal migrants from Bangladesh — who can be handy recruits for ISI." (page 202—205 Will the Iron Fence save a tree hollowed by termites? — Arun Shourie)

The Intelligence Bureau's note from which some excerpts have been quoted above claimed that the number of infilterators from Bangladesh is 15 million (1.5 crore). George Fernandez — former Defence Minister stated in his speech that there number was 20 million (2 crore). Late Inderjeet Gupta " who was also Home Minister , GOI once stated that the number was 10 million (1 crore). Obviously there is no unanimity as to exact the number of such illegal infiltrators. But whatever be the exact number there is no doubt that the number is enormous and their presence in India is fraught with the greatest danger to our national security. The intelligence bureau has clearly mentioned that in the belt running parallel to the border with Bangladesh and significantly deep into Indian Territory, reside a large section of illegal migrants from Bangladesh who can be handy recruits for ISI." Apart from this they also add tremendously to the Muslim population in this country. How has millions of Muslim from Bangladesh managed to infiltrate and comfortably settled themselves in India. Who is responsible for this demographic aggression from Bangladesh?

A quote from the documents of Ministry of External Affairs published in 1963 provide the answers.

"The fact is that enlistment of foreigners in the voters' list has at times taken place at the instance of politically interested persons or parties (Read Congress). Political parties have been known to take dubious steps to inflate the number of their supporters at the election time, and some undoubtedly used the illegal settlers from Pakistan towards this end.

"Many Pakistani nationals who left Tripura themselves stated on return that they had helped, worked and voted for the candidates of a particular political party in India." "These foreigners were no doubt assisted through questionable practices, to have their names on the voters' list. The effort of the aliens has been to accumulate circumstantial evidence since they lacked primary and essential proof of Indian Nationality."

Excerpts from Internal Note prepared by Ministry of Home Affairs, GOI in March 1992:

"It is observed that more and more Muslim immigrants are setting down in the border areas. Accordingly, large stretches of the border in these States are becoming predominantly inhabited by Bangladeshi Muslims. The simmering communal tension in some of the border areas is one of the manifestations of the effects of large scale illegal migration of Bangladeshi nationals who have slowly displaced or dispossessed the local population, particularly those belonging to the Hindu Community, in these areas.

"The Hindu immigrants have been generally staying in shanties in miserable conditions in visible concentration in south West Bengal districts. The Muslim infiltrators have mostly fanned out to urban areas in other States most notably in Delhi, Rajasthan. Gujarat, Maharashtra etc. In the metropolitan cities of Delhi and Bombay not less than 4 to 5 lakh Bangladeshi Muslims have been residing."

"Fact is that the border districts of West Bengal and Assam as also greater Calcutta metropolitan complex have crossed the saturation point in absorbing the immigrants. Employment potential in these areas has become extremely low due to high level of overpopulation. As a result, an ever-increasing number of infiltrators, therefore, after crossing the border move to distant places, i.e. interior districts of West Bengal, Bihar, New Delhi, Bombay, Ahmedabad, Jaipur etc."

"Demographic changes have produced sharply adverse Hindu-Muslim ratio in the population in several border districts in the States adjoining Bangladesh. The influx of illegal migrants who have settled in the border districts in West Bengal, North-Eastern States and Bihar had transformed these districts into overwhelmingly immigrants population districts. The change in the religious composition of population has created socio-economic and religious problems. In as many as 56 Constituencies they have a major electoral voice."

"It would be interesting to note that a group of intellectuals in Dacca is seeking to legitimise the immigration of Muslims into the adjoining areas of North- East region by invoking the theory of lebensraum or living space. A number of Dacca dailies carried articles written on these lines by university professors. They were not at all apologetic about the infiltration. People are sought to be inspired by the hope that one day the north-eastern region will be added to Bangladesh giving it a natural boundary in place of present one which throttles Bangladesh."

"An ideological support is given to the phenomenon by the Islamic fundamentalists creating the vision of a larger Islamic country comprising Bangladesh and the entire North-east where its economic problems will be solved and security ensured."From the above mentioned quotes it will not be wrong to draw the inference that it is the secular forces in India who are responsible for infiltration of Muslim from Bangladesh.

A word about the IMDT Act 1983 would be apposite to have.

It may be recalled that the people of Assam, particularly students mounted a massive agitation in the late seventies seeking expulsion of foreigners from Assam. The unprecedented violence culminated in the most gruesome slaughter of eigtheen hundred Bangladeshis at Nelli by the tribals of Assam. But nothing could induce the mindless government of Assam and India to understand the point of view of Assam students. Assam always had a raw deal at the hands of Govt. of India and national leadership which took no notice of the grievances of Assamese. At the suggestion of the then Chief Minister of Assam Hiteshwar Saikia, the Government of India decided to deal with the problem of detection and deportation of foreigners by establishing tribunals under a new law. The work of drafting this new Act was entrusted to a Muslim advocate Abdul Muhib Mazumdar and not the Ministry of Law who drafted an Act which totally subverted the Constitution of India.

This Act known as Illegal Migrants Detection (Tribunal) Act was an insult to not only the Founding Fathers of the Constitution of India but even the meanest intelligence in the country. This Act was passed by the Parliament on December 12, 1983. So for the first time India had two separate Acts to deal with foreigners. The Indian Foreigners Act 1946 was applicable to the rest of the country while IMDT Act was applicable to Assam only. This Act made it practically impossible for the police to detect and deport any foreigner from Assam. In reality this Act was meant to protect Bangladesh Muslims.

Eminent persons in the country condemned the Act. The Governor of Assam wanted the Act to be repealed. Even the Law Commission recommended its repeal in 2000. As always, the Supreme Court came to the rescue of the nation and declared the Act *ultra vires* of the Constitution.

In an almost devastating judgement, virutally accusing the government of the day of legislative treason towards the nation. The Supreme Court said that "A deep analysis of the IMDT Act and Rules made thereunder would reveal that they have been purposely so enacted or made so as to give shelter or protection to illegal migrants who came to Assam from Bangladesh on or after 25th March 1971 rather than identify or deport them."

Although one of the biggest hurdles in the way of detection and deportation have been removed, millions of illegal infiltrators from Bangladesh continue to stay in Assam. Something will have to be done to make them to go back to their country. India cannot be the allowed to be a victim of a failed state.

13

The Maoist Insurgency in India and Nepal

Prakash Singh

Introduction

The Naxalite movement erupted violently in the country in 1967, its flames spreading to almost all parts of the country. Some of the finest brains and the cream of India's youth in certain areas left their homes and colleges to chase the dream of a new world, a new social order. Two decades had passed since the dawn of independence and yet large segments of the Indian population — peasants, workers and tribals — continued to suffer the worst forms of exploitation. The peaceful political process, it was felt, would not be able to bring about the necessary change because vested interests controlled the levers of power, regulated the wheels of industry and had a feudal stranglehold over the predominantly agrarian economy. An armed struggle was the only way out, they thought.

Naxalbari — Formation of CPI(ML)

It was in such an environment that there was a spark in a small village, Naxalbari, on the tri-junction of India, Nepal and what is today Bangladesh. The Santhals, armed with bows and arrows, forcibly occupied the lands of the kulaks and ploughed them to establish their ownership. Demonstrations were organised against persons holding paddy. In many cases, the entire stocks were lifted and distributed either amongst themselves or sold locally at cheaper rates. There were violent clashes. Between March and May 1967, nearly hundred incidents were reported to the police. The situation progressively deteriorated. After some dithering, the West Bengal government ordered the police to take action. The movement was squashed but, as Samar Sen rightly observed, "Naxalbari exploded many a myth and restored faith in the courage and character of the revolutionary Left in India"[1].

The extremists, following Mao's dictum that "if there is to be revolution, there must be a revolutionary party", formed, on April 22, 1969, the Communist Party of India (Marxist-Leninist). It was declared that

> "...the first and foremost task of our Party is to rouse the peasant masses in the countryside to wage guerilla war, unfold agrarian revolution, build rural base, use the countryside to encircle the cities and finally to capture the cities and to liberate the whole country".

The Author was Director General of Border Security Force. He was also DGP UP and DGP Assam. He was awarded, Padmashri, for his contribution to national security. Singh has written a number of books: *Nagaland, The Naxalite Movement in India, Disaster Response in India and Kohima to Kashmir.*

The Chinese Communist Party welcomed the formation of the CPI(ML). The Marxist-Leninist groups of other countries like UK, Albania and Sri Lanka also extended their recognition. The CPI (ML), in its political resolution, stated that[2].

> *"India is a semi-colonial and semi-feudal country, the principal contradiction in the country is between feudalism and the peasant masses".*

> "The revolutionary situation in India is excellent with the ruling classes enmeshed in economic and political crisis, the party would strive to build a united front of all revolutionary classes, and that guerilla warfare would be the basic tactic of the struggle."

The Flow

The Naxalite movement, drawing inspiration from the Maoist ideology, had a meteoric phase for about two years from the formation of the party till the end of June 1971. The ripples starting from Naxalbari spread in ever-widening circles to practically all parts of the country. The only areas which remained untouched were the North-eastern states and the Union Territories of Goa, Pondicherry and Andaman & Nicobar Islands. The dominant strand of the movement was the annihilation of class enemies. It was Charu Mazumdar's distinctive contribution to the movement. It was his triumph as well as his tragedy — triumph because it achieved a considerable measure of success in the initial stages when several jotedars fled from the countryside and there were tremors among all shades of oppressors, and tragedy because the killings, not always discriminate, alienated the general mass of people and there were serious ideological differences within the party over the formulation which weakened and fragmented the movement.

The annihilation of class enemies was directed at not merely the physical liquidation of a few hated landlords and usurers but at the "overthrow of the feudal class in an area economically, politically and militarily"[3]. It was explained that after the class enemies were annihilated, others of his ilk would also flee in utter panic and the area would be freed of the class enemies and their agents. This would raise the armed struggle to a higher plane. Annihilation of class enemies was viewed as a "higher form of class struggle and the beginning of guerilla war". The annihilation campaign had four basic objectives:[4]

i) smash the feudal authority in the villages and replace it by the authority of the peasants;

ii) establish 'red terror' as opposed to the 'white terror' of feudal elements;

iii) arouse the poor sections of the rural masses to take over the leadership of the movement; and

iv) encourage the common people to shake off their fear and *inertia* to join the Naxalites.

Charu's assessment was that "every corner of India is like a volcano" about to erupt, that "there is the possibility of a tremendous upsurge in India", and he therefore called upon the cadres to start as many points of armed struggle as possible. "Expand anywhere and everywhere" was his message. Such expansions were particularly noticeable in Srikakulam in Andhra Pradesh, Debra-Gopiballavpur in West Bengal, Mushahari in Bihar and Palia in Lakhimpur district of UP.

The Naxalite violence was at peak from about the middle of 1970 to the middle of 1971. Naxalism became a major component in the country's political life. Terrorist violence in different states produced a tremendous impact. The political parties realised the emergence of a new force, the government became conscious of a new threat not only to law and order but to the very existence of the democratic set up in the country, and the people in general either looked forward expectantly or were gripped with a sense of fear depending upon the class they came from or the interests they upheld. It is estimated that there were a total of about 4,000 incidents in the country from the middle of 1970 to the middle of 1971. The bulk of these were from West Bengal (3,500) followed by Bihar (220) and Andhra Pradesh (70). Mazumdar, however, failed to visualise the devastating implications of his approach for the very cause he was trying to champion. Mass movements were neglected, economic struggles did not get due attention and 'white terror' was provoked to launch fierce counter-attacks which nearly decimated the Naxalites. The movement did not have the vital ingredients to sustain itself. No wonder, after attaining a certain trajectory, it showed a downward trend.

The Ebb

The Government of India was forced to take stock of the situation, and it organised joint operations by the army and the police in the bordering districts of West Bengal, Bihar and Orissa which were particularly affected by Naxalite depredations. The operations were undertaken from July 1 to August 15, 1971 and were code-named Operation Steeplechase. The broad strategy of the Security Forces was to surround as large an area as possible and seal the routes of entry and exit. The army formed the outer cordon and the CRPF the inner ring. The local police, which was generally accompanied by a magistrate, carried out thorough search of the area. Suspected Naxalites were arrested, illicit weapons, ammunition and explosives seized. Wherever possible, simultaneous action was taken in the neighbouring area also so that the Naxalites sneaking out were caught while attempting to escape. Such information as was gleaned in the course of operations was followed up by subsequent action. These operations covered Midnapur, Purulia, Burdwan and Birbhum districts of West Bengal; Singhbhum, Dhanbad and Santhal Parganas of Bihar, and Mayurbhanj of Orissa.

The operation achieved the desired results, though not to the extent anticipated by the administration. The organisational apparatus of the Naxalites in the aforesaid districts was thrown out of gear and the party activists fled from their known hideouts to other places in search of safety. Violence registered a drop. Incidents of arms-snatching fell down. Above all, it restored the confidence of the people in the strength of the administration. Charu Mazumdar was also arrested by the Calcutta Police detectives on July 16, 1972. A few days later, he died. Charu's death marked the end of a phase in the Naxalite movement. The period following his death witnessed divisions and fragmentations in the movement.

Revival — PWG

The formation of People's War Group in Andhra Pradesh subsequently in 1980 under the leadership of Kondapalli Seetharamaiah gave a new fillip to the movement. The PWG's program of action included :

- redistribution of land
- enforcing payment of minimum wages to the farm labour
- imposing taxes and penalties
- holding people's courts
- destroying government property

- kidnapping government functionaries
- attacking policemen, and
- enforcing a social code

The PWG is believed to have redistributed nearly half a million acres of land across Andhra Pradesh. Its activists also insisted on a hike in the daily minimum wages and the annual fee for *jeetagadu* (year-long labour). The poorer sections found that what the politicians had been talking about and the government promising year after year could be translated into a reality only with the intervention of Naxalites. *Gorakala* doras (Lord of the Bushes) is how the Naxalites came to be known in the interior areas. Referring to the PWG's grip over the Telengana districts, the editor of *Andhra Frabha* commented as follows[5] :

"....the PWG practically runs a 'parallel government' in Karimnagar, Warangal and Adilabad districts. It collects 'taxes and penalties' from forest and excise contractors, rich landlords and businessmen. It receives complaints from the public, conducts enquiries and investigations, holds people's courts, pronounces judgements, and awards and administers punishments."

Kidnappings to secure the release of its own cadres was frequently resorted to by the PWG activists. The cause celebre was the kidnapping of six IAS officers including a Principal Secretary of the state government and Collector of East Godavari district on December 27, 1987 while they were returning from a tribal welfare meeting at *Pulimatu* in this district. The state government decided to play safe and released the eight Naxalites in Rajahmundry jail. The PWG got tremendous propaganda mileage out of the incident.

The revolutionary writers of the Jana Natya Mandali, the cultural front of the PWG, greatly helped in preparing the environment in which the Naxalite ideology found ready acceptance. Its moving spirit was Gummadi Vittal Rao, better known as Gaddar. He was a balladeer who fought the establishment with the power of his songs. Sample the following[6]:

The Dasshera festival has come

But it is not being celebrated by you.

Deepavali has come
But there are no deepams with you.
Sivaratri has come
And you are observing a fast.
But for you, the whole life is Sivaratri, O Laxmamma
But for you, the whole life is Ammavasi.

The People's War Group gradually spread its organisational network to the coastal and Rayalaseema districts in the state. It extended its tentacles to the adjoining areas of Maharashtra, Madhya Pradesh and Orissa and made a dent even in the bordering districts of Karnataka and certain pockets of Tamilnadu.

The state government banned the PWG and its six front organisations in 1992. At the same time, the state police, assisted by the central paramilitary forces, undertook well-organised counter-insurgency operations. As a result, 248 Naxalites were liquidated and 3,434 activists were apprehended. The arrest of Kondapally Seetharamaiah and other important leaders meant further setback to the PWG.

In Bihar, about the same time, the Maoist Communist Centre perpetrated acts of violence. Its organisational network extended to most of the Central Bihar districts. During the six year period from 1987 to 1992, there were eight major incidents in Gaya, Chatra and Aurangabad districts in which 42 Rajputs, 40 Bhumihars, 5 Muslims, 1 BJP MP and 3 policemen among others were killed. What began as a fight for social and economic justice actually degenerated into a caste conflict with a veneer of class struggle. The MCC ran virtually a parallel judicial system in certain pockets. These were described as Jan Adalat or People's Court where they would shorten an accused by six inches — behead him, in other words!

Present State of Movement

The movement today is in a very fragmented state. There are nearly forty odd groups operating under various labels in different parts of the country, the more important ones being the People's War Group, the Maoist Communist Centre, CPML-Liberation, CPML-Janashakti, CPML-New Democracy, CPML-Red Flag and CPML-Praja Pratighatana.

The heterogeneous Naxalite formation have varying degrees of influence in different states. The CPML (People's War Group) is well entrenched in almost all the districts of Andhra Pradesh, several districts of central and south Bihar, southern districts of Madhya Pradesh and Orissa and a couple of eastern districts of Maharashtra. The group has registered its presence in some districts of Karnataka, Tamilnadu and West Bengal also. The MCC is formidable in about 11 districts of south Bihar and 9 districts of central Bihar. The group has made inroads into Madhya Pradesh as well. The CPML-Liberation has a conspicuous presence in 28 districts of Bihar, 6 districts of West Bengal and in parts of Assam, Andhra Pradesh, Gujarat, Karnataka, Rajasthan and UP. The CPML-Janashakti is active mainly in the Telengana area of Andhra Pradesh. The CPML-New Democracy has pockets of influence in Andhra Pradesh and Bihar. The other groups have nominal presence like CPML-Red Flag in Kerala and CPML-Praja Pratighatana in Andhra Pradesh.

All the Naxalite formations taken together have a strength of about 10,000 underground and 40,000 overground cadres. Besides, the various front organisations of the Left Wing Extremist groups have about 1 lac activists. The formations have a sizeable arsenal, and are believed to be in possession of at least 10,000 weapons which include more than 200 AK-47 rifles and about 250 SLRs apart from other weapons like sten guns, carbines, assorted rifles and a huge stock of explosives. Some groups, particularly the PWG and the MCC, have acquired expertise in the preparation and use of IEDs.

No wonder, the Naxalites pack considerable lethal punch. They have been killing 500 to 600 persons every year. According to figures with the Home Ministry, in 1999 there were 1,246 incidents of Left extremist violence in which 598 people were killed and property worth Rs. 6 crore was destroyed. In 2000, 550 people were killed and property worth Rs. 8 crore was destroyed. And, in 2001, 554 people were annihilated and property worth a whopping Rs. 25 crore was destroyed across the country. Andhra Pradesh is the worst affected state accounting for about 40% of the total Naxalite violence in the country followed by Jharkhand, Bihar, Chhattisgarh, Eastern Uttar Pradesh, Maharashtra, Madhya Pradesh, Orissa and West Bengal.

In Andhra Pradesh, the PWG has set up a People's Guerilla Army "to strengthen the political power of the people and to defeat the efforts of the State and the Central Governments to check the (revolutionary) movement". On the first anniversary of its formation, the outfit blew up factories owned by the Chief Minister Chandrababu Naidu's family and Union Minister Krishnam Raju in Chittoor district. The PWG has even formed State/Zonal/sub-Zonal military commands and raised several military platoons. The effort obviously is to militarise the armed wing of the PWG so that it is able to take on the police and the paramilitary forces. It is estimated that the PWG is able to collect about Rs. 10 crore every year to finance its expenses on the purchase of weapons and other equipments.

Peace talks were held between the People's War Group and the State Government of Andhra Pradesh recently at the initiative of Committee of Concerned Citizens. Three rounds of talks were held but unfortunately there was no agreement on the substantive issues. The PWG called off the talks in July 2002 in protest against the state police continuing to kill their cadres in 'fake encounters'.

In Jharkhand, there were 267 Naxalite related incidents in 1999 involving 176 deaths; and, in 2000, there were 318 incidents involving 193 deaths. The MCC and the PWG account for bulk of the incidents. Interestingly, there are inter-party clashes also for area hegemony. There were 29 such clashes in 2000 in which 46 members of different groups lost their lives.

In Bihar, Naxalite violence registered an increase from 214 incidents in 1999 to 278 incidents in 2000. The corresponding figures of casualties were, however, 202 and 170. The MCC was responsible for about half the total number of incidents. There are clashes between the various Naxalite outfits and also between Senas and the Naxalite formations. The MCC has been quite brazen in its attack on police posts.

In Chhattisgarh, Naxalite violence is concentrated mainly in Bastar area and in Rajnandgaon, Jashpur and Sarguja districts. Eastern Uttar Pradesh has witnessed stirrings of Naxalite activities in Sonbhadra, Gorakhpur, Ghazipur, Ballia and Mirzapur districts. In Maharashtra, Gadchiroli is particularly affected, though there are incidents in Bhandara, Chandrapur, Gondia and Nanded districts also. In Madhya Pradesh, following the bifurcation of the state, Naxalite violence is confined to Balaghat district only. Orissa witnessed a qualitative increase in Naxalite violence during 2000 and 2001. The MCC has established its presence in the northern districts while the PWG has consolidated itself in the southern districts. The formation of Andhra-Orissa Border Special Zonal Committee has given fillip to Left Wing Extremism in the State.

Naxalite violence in West Bengal is at a low pitch compared to the other states. This is to be attributed to the success of Operation Barga under which sharecroppers were registered and given permanent and inheritable rights on cultivation of their plots covering a total area of 11 lac acres. Besides, 1.37 lac acres of ceiling surplus and benami lands were acquired by the state government and distributed among 25 lac landless and marginal cultivators. The land reforms have seen the emergence of a new class loosely termed 'rural rich' and weakened the social and political power enjoyed by the landlords in the countryside.

Nexus

The Naxalite groups' nexus with the other extremist organizations has added to the complexity of the problem. There are indications that the PWG cadres received training in the handling of weapons and IEDs from some ex-LTTE cadres. They have also some kind of understanding with the NSCN(IM) for supporting each others' cause. The CPML-Party Unity had agreed to undertake propaganda campaign in favour of the ULFA and the latter had agreed to reciprocate the gesture. Some batches of CPML-PU perhaps also received arms training under the guidance of ULFA. The PWG and the MCC also appear to have worked out a strategic alliance with the Communist Party of Nepal (Maoist).

Prospects

The factors which gave rise to Naxalism in the country are, unfortunately, very much present today also — and in an acute and aggravated form. The extent of poverty in the country continues to be abysmal. According to a paper prepared jointly by K.Sundaram and Suresh Tendulkar[8], both professors at the Delhi School of Economics, rural poverty did not decline at all in the 1990s. This was because of high foodgrain prices and a deceleration in value-addition in agriculture. The reduction in poverty during 1981-91, according to them, resulted predominantly from agricultural growth and not from expanded coverage of the anti-poverty programs.

It has been rightly said that the Naxalite movement, fed by rural deprivation, is significantly different from the violent agitations in Punjab and Assam in the past. "It is based neither on religious fundamentalism nor on any sense of regional or linguistic injustice. Sustained by the theory of class struggle, Naxalite extremism, therefore, is unlikely to die down with the ebbing of any momentary madness. Linked to social and economic inequities, it is clearly more durable than a fundamentalist campaign. So long as feudal exploitation continues and the local administration sides with the affluent landlords in their dispute with the landless poor, the cause for such ultra-left extremism will exist.[9]"

Meanwhile, the merger of the Peoples War and the Maoist Communist Centre of India, the two most powerful components of the Naxalite movement in the country, on May 21, 2004 to form the Communist Party of India (Maoist) is likely to give greater thrust and momentum to the movement in the coming years.

The erosion of faith in the political process, economic disparities, mounting unemployment, tribal unrest, aggravating social tensions and the failure of administration to fulfill the rising expectations of the people are all leading to a highly explosive situation. The government, tragically, continues to deal with these as law and order problem only. It is treating the symptoms and not the disease. The powers that we have yet to realise that unless the basic issues are addressed, the exploited, the deprived and the alienated will continue to protest — and some of them opt for the path of armed struggle — to change the system.

Maoist Movement in Nepal

The Maoist movement in Nepal is essentially a reaction to the political instability in the country, the socio-economic inequalities in the countryside and the rampant corruption in the bureaucracy. There are even today areas where there are no schools, no roads, no electricity and no medical facilities. At the national level, the number of educated unemployed is increasing every year. The Maoist's were initially part of the communist movement in Nepal but, in 1996, they broke away and formed a separate Communist Party of Nepal-Maoist (CPN-Maoist). They drew inspiration from Peru's Shining Path and submitted a forty-point charter of demands to the government of Nepal, demanding abolition of the monarchy and setting up of a multi-party democracy based on Marxist principles.

The Maoists declared 'People's War' when their demands were turned down by the government. They have gradually spread their influence to about 40 districts out of the total of 75 districts in the country. The CPN(M) has a well-defined organisational structure comprising a politburo and a central committee followed by regional bureaus, district and area committees. The armed wing has a central military commission with military commands at the district level. The total strength of the Maoists is about 15,000 out of which 2,000 are armed cadres. Dr. Baburam Bhattarai is the chief ideologue of the party while Pushpa Kamal Dahal, better known by his alias Prachanda (The Fierce), is the head of the armed wing.

There has been a running battle between the Maoist rebels and the Nepalese Police with heavy casualties on both sides. After Deuba took over as Prime Minister (July 26, 2001), there were peace talks between the representatives of the government and the Maoist leaders. Three rounds of talks were held, but the Maoist withdrew and resumed violence on November 23, 2001. The government retaliated by imposing emergency and deploying the Royal Nepal Army. It also enacted a Terrorists and Violating Work (Control & Punishment) ordinance which contained provisions imposing severe restrictions on the media including limitations on "insulting" the king and royal family as well as any "news encouraging the Maoists to involve in terror". It is estimated that the insurgency in Nepal has taken a toll of about 10,000 people so far since 1996.

The Communist Party of Nepal (Maoist) has been able to forge links with the communist revolutionaries of Peru, Philippines and India. The party has very close fraternal links with the People's War Group and the Maoist Communist Centre of India. There are indications that they have struck a relationship with the LTTE of Sri Lanka also.

The Nepal Maoists' links with the Naxalite outfits of India have a dangerous security dimension. They plan to carve out a Compact Revolutionary Zone (CRZ) comprising areas under the influence of the CPN(Maoist) in Nepal with those of the MCC (in Bihar and Jharkhand) and the CPML-PW (in Andhra Pradesh and Chhattisgarh). The Nepalese Maoists are also using India as a sanctuary. Pressure from the Nepalese security forces compels them to flee across the border and move into the contiguous areas, particularly of Bihar and Eastern UP. The immigrant Nepali organisations like the Akhil Bharat Nepali Ekta Samaj, Akhil Bharat Nepali Vidyarthi Sangh and Akhil Bharat Nepali Mahila Samaj have come to notice for helping the Nepalese Maoists. Some of these Maoists have been apprehended in UP, Bihar, West Bengal, Delhi, Uttaranchal and Sikkim and deported back to Nepal.

There was another interlude of peace from October 20 to 28, 2004 for the *Dashain* festival. However, soon after the security forces and the Maoists clashed again in Dang district on October 29. On February 1, 2005, in a sudden move, King Gyanendra sacked Prime Minister Deuba, grabbed absolute power and declared a state of emergency, charging the ruling coalition of failing to hold talks with the Maoist rebels and conduct parliamentary elections. This led a popular agitation in the course of which the Maoists joined hands with the seven agitating political parties. The King had to ultimately relent and restore the parliament on April 24, 2006. The party leaders thereupon elected G.P. Koirala as the Prime Minister. Now Maoist Chief Prachanda and Prime Minister G.P. Koirala have signed The Comprehensive Peace Agreement under which Maoists have agreed to subject themselves to the law of the land. It has paved the way for the induction of the Maoists in the interim Govt.

The Government of India has offered a massive economic package to help Nepal rebuild its economy. India would, however, have to be very careful to guard its strategic interests in Nepal. For this, it will have to ensure that :

the democratic experiment in Nepal succeeds

development schemes are sincerely implemented

perceptions of Indian hegemony being removed

the nexus between Nepalese Maoists and the Indian Naxalite groups is broken, and

the ISI network in Nepal is systematically countered.

References

1. Samar Sen, *Naxalbari and After, A Frontier Anthology*, Foreword.
2. *Naxalbari and After, A Frontier Anthology,* Vol.II pp.251-263.
3. *Liberation*, September-December 1970, p.22
4. Biplab Dasgupta, *Economic and Political Weekly*, Annual Number, 1973, pp.173-187
5. Terror in Telengana, *Indian Express*, Aug. 13, 1989
6. Prakash Singh, *The Naxalite Movement in India*, p.105
7. *Times of India*, Jan.9, 2002
8. Jairam Ramesh, *India Today*, July 31, 2000, p.40
9. Bhaskar Roy, *Times of India*, July 11, 2002

14

Chasing Shadows: Sub-Conventional Warfare — Doctrinal Issues

Brig. Kiran Krishan, SM (Retd.)

> *"On September 10, 2001, there was not the slightest hint that the United States was about to embark on an all-out campaign against 'global terrorism'.... The business-as-usual approach to foreign policy vanished on September 11."*
>
> — Stephen M. Walt[1]

The New Age Scourge

"The borders have dissolved. There are no front lines. There are no non-combatants. Our defenses begin abroad but do not end at our borders. Our defenses must continue within our territory. Our foes operate not on conventional battlefields but in a gray area where traditional notions of crime and armed conflict overlap," writes Brian Michael Jenkins, one of the world's leading authorities on international terrorism, and senior adviser to the president of the RAND Corporation, Santa Monica, USA.[2] Modern day terrorism poses a potent challenge to the very concept of conventional war, tied as it is to territory and military objectives defined in terms of its capture, or attrition to enemy manpower and equipment. Often, neither the enemy is visible, nor his objectives certain.

What were Osama bin Laden's objectives in the 9/11 outrages — demonstrating vulnerability of America — frightening the United States — mete punishment to America[3] — revitalising Islamic ideology? The problem does not stop there. How do the terrorists measure their success, or define victory? Was 9/11 a success from terrorists' point o view? And, how should the state measure success in its war against this new age war — number of terrorists killed and captured—number of attacks prevented or, stanching terrorist ideology? For long atomic weapons and connected rhetoric was a means to conducting international relations. Does terrorism portend to become the new star, the dominant idiom of internatio.ial discourse?

Politically violent movements beneath the threshold of conventional war have been a pervasive feature in human history. Variously identified in different epochs as guerrilla war, insurrection, rebellion, revolution, internal war, irregular war, unconventional war, and lately as terrorism, those engaging in insurgency, asymmetric warfare or terrorism, as "sub-state actors", often with the aid and abetment of inimical states, or other transnational forces have always posed strong challenge to the existing political order. It is implicit in that argument that it is almost impossible to eradicate political violence altogether.

Contemporary terrorism derives from that tradition, and has developed along innovative lines, combining modern weapons and explosives, information and communications, technologies, and worldwide mobility, with highly flexible, decentralised cellular organisational forms, underpinned by ideology. The events of September 11, 2001 have demonstrated their capability to exponentially scale the impact of their attacks within existing means. Could they acquire Weapons of Mass Destruction (WMD)? Lieutenant General BS Malik avers that they certainly can, "*Firstly,* terrorists may take over a state having nuclear weapons.... *Secondly,* the supporters of terrorism as a policy tool in a nuclear state, due reasons of domestic conflict may covertly help the terrorists to acquire fissile material for making a crude dirty bomb."[4]

Sub-conventional War

The term "Sub-conventional War" encapsulates Low Intensity Conflict (LIC), and terrorism as commonly understood, and its more esoteric forms using innovative techniques, WMD, high technology, cyber attacks etc. Israel's Minister without Portfolio Dan Meridor is credited with coining the term "Sub-conventional Warfare". Meridor feels, "in view of Israel's significant edge in conventional warfare, the Arabs have shifted to warfare at two levels. The *first* level, which can be called supra-conventional (emphasis by writer), involves the development of nuclear, biological and chemical weapons. The *second* level, which can be called sub-conventional (emphasis by writer), expresses itself in non-conventional terrorism."[5]

He offers examples of non-conventional terrorism: "Let us assume that someone creates a serious malfunction in the control system of a railway. As a result, trains crash into each other and in this single mass terrorist act, 50,000 persons lose their lives. Or, for example, a terrorist incident can turn the entire oxygen system in a nation's hospitals haywire." The conclusion Meridor offered was that the Israel Defence Forces (IDF) must reformulate their theory of combat in dealing with a threat in which planes, tanks and precision-guided weapons constituted an inadequate solution.[6] The IDF now consider sub-conventional war a major strategic challenge and are gradually transforming from a force designed to fight short conventional wars into a military adapted for managing a continuous Low-Intensity Conflict (LIC) and various mutations of terrorism.

Does India need a fresh look at the surge in this worldwide scourge, and re-engineer its responses? In the ensuing survey, an attempt has been made to answer this and allied questions. While endeavour has been made to establish the need of sub-conventional warfare doctrine and its major contours, it is not possible to enunciate doctrine in a short essay. But, first there is a need to understand the modern manifestations of sub-conventional war and examine the Indian experience.

Understanding Sub-conventional War Nuclear Factor: Many analysts attribute emergence of terrorism as a preferred mode of resolving conflict to the advent of nuclear weapons — the fear that a conventional war may escalate to nuclear war. The terrorists and states sponsoring terrorism, sensing the redundancy of WMDs, and inability to wage conventional war have moved in the available space. Air Commodore Jasjit Singh writes, "The significant point to note is that in the past, wars of the sub-continent were limited (in time, space, goals, etc.) by choice. But nuclearisation has made wars limited as an imperative."[7] Of course, the definition of limited war itself could be changing. How limited it is, depends largely on how the contestants view it.

Redefining War: The purpose of conventional war by a state usually is to impose its will on the adversary state, and this is sought to be achieved by occupying territory and destruction of men and equipment. Sub-conventional war seeks to achieve the same purpose by LIC and spectacular acts of violence followed by manipulation of fear psychosis. However, the very concept of "imposition of will" could be changing. A particular terrorist act may not be linked to any immediate and discernible tangible gains. International terrorism has a dynamic of its own. It does not respect national and international laws, or recognise the authority of states. The entities and individual actors in today's sub-conventional war could be from any country and their agenda might straddle many states and range from extracting economic concessions, taking over diamond mines to overturning governments, or just sending across an ideological message.

State sponsors: Terrorism is not restricted to sub-state groups alone. The locus often traverses state actors, carefully camouflaged, and sometime rather open and blatant as with Pakistan's "war of thousand cuts against India". Could an operation like 9/11 have been mounted without active help of some state actor? Was there a state sponsor—hidden behind the terrorist screen—often implied, seldom explicitly stated, and as yet unproven? Was Pakistan's A.Q. Khan selling nuclear secrets and materials all on his own! Many terrorist groups in India's North-east are openly operating from camps located inside Bangladesh.

Mutation of Terrorism

Post Second World War, sub-conventional war was largely of two varieties — random acts of violence followed by active guerrilla wars of liberation. Often both existed simultaneously, one reinforcing the other. The effects were largely localised. Stand-alone spectacular acts of terror entered the repertoire in the1960s with hijacking of civil airliners, assassinations, and massacres etc. The tactical corner stones for such stand-alone acts were "high voltage drama" and "publicity" followed by manipulation of fear through media play for highlighting the terrorist cause and extracting specific concessions.[8] The massacre of Israeli athletes in Munich in 1972 falls in this category. However, 9/11 is a category apart. After the 9/11 attacks, Israeli Minister Dan Meridor commented: "Osama bin Laden [has] carried out the kind of attack that has been depicted in suspense films. I still cannot fully digest what happened over there. Unfortunately, this attack is only the beginning."[9] This catastrophic event has demonstrated the exponential increase in the terrorist reach, ambitions, and brought terrorism nearly *at par* with war. The possibility of terrorists using WMD can no longer be discounted.[10] Modern day terrorism has mutated into a major strategic challenge for world governments.

Globalisation of Terror

Like globalisation of politics and economics, there is globalisation of terror. Effects of spectacular terrorist are felt instantly across the globe. The horror of awe-inspiring images of 9/11 beamed across the world in real time couldn't have failed to touch world audiences. While policy-makers would have been reinforced in their motivation to extirpate terrorism, perhaps, the images also inspired Indian terrorists to mount spectacular attacks on the J&K Assembly in October 2001 and the Indian Parliament in December 2001. Economic globalisation assists instant and anonymous transfer of large amounts of money, the primary lubricant of international terrorism. Nexus between arms dealers, criminals, and terrorists is now an established reality. In December 2004, two criminals carrying 253.6 gm of Uranium were arrested by police near Bareilly.[11] Recently, the US Federal Bureau of Investigation (FBI) arrested Hekmet Lakhani, a British national of Indian origin for smuggling a sophisticated Russian missile system into the country.[12] The director of the FBI had earlier testified before the US House of Representatives International Relations Committee on Global Terrorism and Organised Crime that international narcotics dealings generated a profit of $ 400 billion, representing approximately eight per cent of the world economy. He expressed his concern about interest of organised crime in nuclear missile materials.[13] Global network and reach of Al Qaeda is an acknowledged reality. Though, currently it is almost *de rigueur* to think of international terror in Islamic terms, there are mercenaries doing the rounds to do the will of the highest bidder.[14]

Technology and Terrorism

The Revolution in Military Affairs (RMA) riding on the wave of modern technologies, improved transportation, weapons, explosives, microelectronics, information and communication systems — while revolutionising conventional warfare has not left the non-conventional warrior untouched. It has caused a "revolution in terrorist affairs" as well. *The New York Times* columnist Thomas Friedman talks of the emergence of the "super-empowered individual": "The individual has been empowered in an unprecedented way to do things he could never do before. Someone can sit on an island in Indonesia and, with a computer, can access the world's knowledge, conduct international commercial transactions, or issue orders.

Previously, countries fought countries. Now groups fight countries, individual fight countries; it is a different type of game altogether."[15] Modern technology has enabled terrorists to establish worldwide network(s) of autonomous and, semi-autonomous terrorist groups and infrastructure amenable to central control and quick response. Modern technology helps terrorists as much as the state forces—without the restraint of national and international laws.

The Indian Experience

Despite impeccable democratic credentials, India has continuously been home to insurgency in one state or the other, ever since her independence. She has also had to contend with significant acts of terrorism, particularly since the 1980s when Sikh militants took to attacking government officials and citizens. Mrs. Indira Gandhi, the then Prime Minister of India, was assassinated by her Sikh security guards on October 31, 1984. In 1985, to tackle the growing menace of terrorism, India raised a specialised counter-terrorist force, the National Security Guard (NSG). India was seldom taken seriously by the world in her protestations. The West, particularly America always took an overly didactic tone towards India. To an extent 9/11 opened a window of opportunity for India for obtaining international cooperation. Post 9/11 the world is lot more cognisant of Indian concerns.

America responded to 9/11 by launching regime change and pre-emption wars against Afghanistan and Iraq. America has also created a separate Department for Homeland Security (DHS) in addition to existing law enforcement and security agencies for protection of the American mainland. How has India been responding to the challenge?

Counter-Insurgency: Despite India's long experience, except the Mizo and Punjab insurgencies; none other has been brought to a favourable conclusion. India's oldest problem — the Naga insurgency — continues to simmer even today, despite the grant of statehood to Nagaland in 1963. Today practically the entire North-east of the country is in the grip of terrorism.[16] "Assam's two hill districts— Karbi Anglong and North Cachar— have both turned into a haven for militant groups.... Officials admit in private that all of them pay a 'tax' to the underground groups."[17] Naxalite armed rebellion that had erupted in 1967 in West Bengal's Naxalbari village, and was crushed— continues even today despite numerous crackdowns over decades and has spread to many other states.[18] In October 2003, fifty-five districts in nine states were affected by Naxalite activity. By November 2004, one hundred and fifty-six districts spread across 13 states were covered by the movement.[19] J&K continues to remain on boil. If anything, over the years, active insurgencies across the country have multiplied manifold.

High Profile Terrorism: Indian Army has been roundly criticised for ham-handed handling of the 1984 Operation Blue Star. Lately, criticism has come from none other than P C Alexander, Principal Secretary to Mrs. Indira Gandhi during the critical period. Alexander writes in his recent book, *Through the Corridors of Power* that "the Army was poorly informed about what awaited them inside the Golden Temple".[20] Brahma Chellany has called the Indian response to the 1999 Kandahar hijack of Flight IC-814 "abominable grovelling" and comments: "In the aftermath of the Kandahar cave-in, cross-border terrorism morphed from hit-and-run attacks to daring assaults on military camps and national emblems of power, like Parliament and Red Fort."[21] The unconsummated *Operation Parakram,* ten month long mobilisation of the Indian Armed Forces could hardly be considered a well thought out and calibrated response to the December 13, 2001 terrorist attack on the Indian Parliament. Former Army Chief, General Shankar Roychowdhury has called the operation a "strategic disaster"[22]

Need for National Policy and Doctrinal Framework

Post 9/11, from being a sideshow, terrorism has moved centrestage, and for good reasons. Co-operation to beat international terrorism heads the discussion agenda wherever heads of states and statesmen meet today. Jaswant Singh, India's former Foreign and Finance Minister respectively in the National Democratic Alliance (NDA) Government (1999-2004) writes, "In the transformed nature of war what India is experiencing and shall have to contend with is not so much open, direct conflict as covert war, clandestine war.... In turn this altered and transformed nature of war will require a total transformation of our concepts and response mechanisms too."[23] Ergo, the main challenge the country faces in the near future is from sub-conventional warfare and not an all-out conventional war.

To craft doctrine to adequately meet the terrorist challenge in its various manifestations, lessons from Punjab and Mizoram success stories as also perceived shortcomings in handling of major incidents need to be taken on board. K. P. S. Gill, formerly the Director General Punjab Police, who more than anyone else is credited for bringing Punjab back from the terrorist abyss, writes that it was a myth that terrorism in Punjab was defeated, not by Police action, not by the force of arms, but because it simply lost popular support.[24] He remains a staunch proponent of suppression of terrorism by declaring war on terrorism. He feels, "It is a perversity to think that terrorism does, in some sense, represent the 'democratic will'; that it expresses—possibly by illegitimate means—the legitimate aspirations of the people; and that, when the political agenda of the masses somehow...changes, terrorism simply 'withers away, or the terrorists adopt the methods and objectives sanctioned by the masses. Nothing could be more patently absurd."[25] In Mizoram, strict population and movement control measures on the lines of the British counter-insurgency experience in Malaya, including setting up of 'progressive protective villages' where population, specially in isolated sectors was grouped together in one village and placed under effective administration, and protection did play a stellar role in bringing round the insurgents.[26]

As for the Army's handling of Operation Blue Star, Alexander ought to know better. The Army was brought in at the last moment, as the state's "instrument of last resort". Throughout the Punjab terrorist saga prior to the operation, the state was in a denial mode and tolerated defiance of law to the extent that in April 1983, A S Atwal, Deputy Inspector General, Punjab Police, was murdered by Bhindranwale goons outside the Golden Temple, and no action was taken. Would Army have done better had it been involved with Punjab affairs earlier? Certainly! Another fundamental of anti-terror operations is continuous collection, evaluation, and timely dissemination of intelligence. The Punjab Police should have provided accurate intelligence to the Army. Besides, shouldn't the Army have asked for more time to fill in the intelligence picture? In comparison, Operation Black Thunder launched on May 18, 1988 was a success when these conditions were met. At the time of December 1999 Kandahar hijack, the Indian Army Chief was neither a member of the National Crisis Management Group nor was he invited to attend its deliberations. The Army help wasn't asked for, and spurned when offered. The Army Chief on his own had moved two infantry companies to the airfield at Amritsar. These were neither used nor associated with the anti-hijack operation.[27] Could India have launched an Entebbe like rescue mission, undertaken by the IDF on the night of July 3, 1976 that successfully rescued Israeli passengers taken to Entebbe (Uganda) in a hijacked Air France plane? In 1999, the NSG, India's premier counter-terrorism force responsible for anti-hijack operations had been in existence for 14 years, but even the basic coordination procedures had not been taped up. A force is only as effective as those employing it. As for the controversial Operation Parakram, necessary intellectual framework for meaningful evaluation of all aspects of escalation didn't appear to be in place. This is a matter for the historians to unravel.

India's handling of sub-conventional conflicts would appear to suffer from *ad hoc* responses, crafted as the situations developed rather than the handiwork of a firm controlling mind fortified by policy, diligently formulated, and executed through institutional mechanisms. The results bear the imprint of political oddballs, mostly without security training, assorted bureaucrats, policemen, and soldiers improvising and pooling resources as the situations developed rather than being pro-active. *There is an urgent need to establish policy guidelines and a doctrinal framework.*

National Policy

While addressing the Combined Commanders' Conference at New Delhi, on November 1, 2003, the then Prime Minister Atal Behari Vajpayee "stressed that India should stay focussed on evolving a 'comprehensive counter-terrorism doctrine backed by suitable capabilities of manpower and high-technology equipment' given its continued exposure to Pakistan's proxy war against it."[28] It needs to be acknowledged that the twin problems of insurgency and terrorism are here to stay for a while.

The debate on shaping national policies for combating sub-conventional war against the Indian state has followed two strands:

War on Terrorism Approach. This calls for development of government competencies to conduct war against terrorism by all available means, unimpeded by restraints of law and accepts curtailment of liberties as a necessity for guarding civil rights.

Liberalist Political Approach. No compromise on civil liberties and no concessions to security agencies at the expense of civil rights.

"The national policy has been to permit no secession of any area under any circumstances. Any problem will have to be solved within the framework of the Constitution. Wherever possible, the problem should be tackled through a democratic Government in the State, by providing it all the possible assistance and making it accountable," writes General K. V. Krishna Rao (Retd), former Chief of Army Staff (COAS) and, Governor of J&K respectively.[29] The Group of Ministers (GoM) Report (2001)[30] has made several recommendations for toning up internal security. The report recognises the need for all pillars of the state viz. the Legislature, the Executive, and the Judiciary to act in concert, and emphasises the paramount importance of maintaining the civil face of Government, even while the Armed Forces of the Union are deployed in aid of civil authority, and stresses that clear cut procedures and unambiguous legal backing be provided to the Armed Forces, to enable them to operate effectively when called upon to assist civil authorities. The report asks for strengthening existing laws, repealing redundant laws, and more authority for the Centre to intervene in the States and calls for affecting improvements in the functioning of the state police forces and Central Police Organisations (CPOs). An important recommendation of the report having a direct bearing on the conduct of anti-insurgency operations is: "Whenever the functioning of two or more Armed Forces is involved, there should be no ambiguity whatsoever, in the chain of operational command. Thus, where the Army is involved, the senior most Army officer should have the clear responsibility and authority, for all operational planning and execution. Clear instructions may be issued in this regard."[31]

A part of the polity sees terrorists as mirror images of our own selves, though misguided, nevertheless a part of our own body and soul, to be approached in the spirit of conciliation and given all legal protections under the laws of the land. Veteran journalist Kuldip Nayar discussing the recent upsurge in Naxalite terrorism in Andhra Pradesh laments, " The Naxalites are treated as criminals, not rebels.... Seldom has the government gone into the real cause of social unrest or uprising.... The remedy is not additional security forces or more repressive laws but the realisation that conciliation can replace confrontation.[32] Noam Chomsky, noted American thinker writes, "Two different issues need to be studied, the issue of 'legality' and the issue of 'justice'. The first is a technical question of law and history...the second question is more elusive — it is the question of proper standards."[33]

Arun Shourie asserts terrorism must be treated as war, and "Wars are won by overpowering the opponent with overwhelming force. And so it must be in the case of terrorism, and of the States that sponsor it: not 'an eye for an eye, a tooth for a tooth'; but for an eye, both eyes, for a tooth, the whole jaw." He continues, "No war has been won by deploying 'minimum force'—the quantum that liberals concede when the terrorist leaves them no option but to accept that something just has to be done."[34]

Though, not all across the political spectrum are in agreement, the dominant political view appears to verge on compassion towards terrorists and insurgents—a marked preference for "winning hearts and minds" over the "war on terrorism" approach. Is there a dominant military view? There are mixed opinions but the Indian Army is a professional apolitical force and the prevalent government view has found echo in the Indian Army Chief, General J. J. Singh's recent exhortation to the Army to give a humane touch to its anti-terror drive.[35] It is evident that no single approach is likely to work. Response crafted by the state of necessity has to be an eclectic mix of both the approaches.

Evolution of National Sub-conventional War Doctrine: At the macro level, the Indian state has selected the democratic form of governance—that gives free play to all shades of political forces, to share power and dissolve ethnic, religious, regional and economic tensions in the Indian democratic melting pot, as its preferred conflict resolution mechanism. The larger doctrinal model that India has provided for is "restoration of democratic rule" in the states and "letting the state governments handle terrorist and insurgent situations" with the mandate of the people behind them. India has persisted with this model with mixed results.

Practically, all sub-conventional wars have underlying political motives. Hans Morgenthau, renowned world authority on international politics writes that "politics is the concept of interest defined on terms of power."[36] Sub-conventional conflict is a ploy to create conditions for either seizing power, or bargaining for a share in it. Thomas Schelling opines, "To study the strategy of conflict is to take the view that most conflict situations are essentially bargaining situations...."[37]

Recognising this basic facet of sub-conventional war, the state should endeavour to transform the disputants' perceptions of the state's intentions, and its ability to overcome conflict. Thus, creating favourable conditions for binding political negotiations should be the primary aim of the state. How can this be done? Richard K Betts observes, "...the fundamental issue in a war (especially in ethnic conflict) is almost always 'Who rules when the fighting stops?'...therefore, wars do not begin unless both parties in a dispute prefer to fight than concede, and as a corollary, wars do not end 'until both sides agree who will control whatever is in dispute'[38]. It is mainly because of these reasons that critics suggest that the best chance to halt hostilities, with or without external third-party intervention is when a conflict is 'ripe'. In other words, the prospects for peace are at their brightest when a conflict is at a stage of 'hurting stalemate', where adversaries are exhausted and have come to believe that little can be gained by further prolonging and escalating the conflict."[39]

Manipulation is not the policy: Bibhu Prasad Routray comments, "Among the recurrent principles that emerge from the various theatres of insurgency across India is the fact that terrorist groups seldom negotiate unless they have been pushed to the wall — and even in these circumstances, they often engage in negotiations as a tactic to buy time to regroup."[40] Armed groups attempting to gain political control of a state engage in a highly complex political-psychological war. Some Indian policy-makers appear married to the idea of 'bringing back the boys' by the simple expedient of buying off the insurgent leadership and cadres.[41] Whereas the aim of state efforts has to be to bring round the terrorists to the negotiating table, negotiations from a position of perceived weakness are unlikely to succeed. Strategy crafted by the state must not be sick of weakness masquerading as munificence. Manipulation is not policy. Individuals can be manipulated but organisations seldom can. Terrorists will come round when they are roundly defeated or perceive that they can gain nothing more by violence, and it has started hurting their public support and cause.

The state's 'conflict management design' must be pro-active and span the entire distance to include: conflict prevention; conflict management; conflict resolution; and peace building. It has to be built around the principles of: good governance; prophylaxis— an ounce of prevention than cure; anticipation and early warning — through regular evaluation and intelligence; constant political and military risk assessment; continuous engagement— at multiple levels of central and state governments across complete range of government activities, political parties, interested social groups and NGOs both formally and informally; international cooperation— to close down foreign sanctuaries, stanching flow of arms, mercenaries and money; timely decision on use of military force; negotiations— timing, design, content and authority to break or continue; and finally, media management.

The fatal flaw in the Indian system has been the absence of a conflict management design—lack of coordinated effort, and too much reliance on one instrument of the government at any one time operating in isolation—cutting shady intelligence deals, economic largesse without absorption mechanisms and effective supervision, premature negotiations with disparate groups without ensuring the 'ripeness' of the conflict, bringing in military late—using a sledge hammer where a fly whisk would have worked, diplomacy without backing of force and, at times, downright political skulduggery. Its end moods have swung between euphoria and despair. Statecraft does not imply cutting deals alone. There is also a vacuous notion that intelligence services hold the key to sub-conventional conflict. Integration of all government agencies and diplomatic efforts to craft international cooperation is the *sine qua non* for effective response by the state.

Post December 13, 2001 terrorist attack on the Indian Parliament, the Indian Government contemplated launching an attack against Pakistan. Whereas, limited war cannot be discounted as a device to deal with transnational terrorism, if Indian experience of Operation Parakram be any guide, such decisions have major long-term ramifications, and must be debated thoroughly as part of doctrinal development with all the implications thought through. Similarly, unless the country is willing to take serious retaliation in its stride, cross border raids cannot be thought to serve a useful purpose. On April 17, 2001, 16 BSF jawans were killed at Boraibari in a border clash with Bangladesh Rifles and villagers. "According to Indian newspaper reports, the 16 soldiers killed were part of a four-company strong force of 400 men sent into Bangladesh territory on 'an ill-conceived mission that had been cleared, according to BSF sources, at the highest political level'."[42] Use of military force in the transborder context cannot be an option unless the country is prepared to go the whole hog. It is not possible for India to replicate American policy options, besides possessing overwhelming economic and military muscle; it is protected by two oceans, the Atlantic and Pacific.

The new forms of high profile or catastrophic stand-alone terror acts, WMD related terrorism and hi-tech terrorism such as cyber war etc. are a case apart and need to be carefully debated with the help of specialists and dedicated organisations need to be raised. Special care is required about crisis management teams—these cannot be the domain of generalist alone. All sources must be tapped. "Publicity is the oxygen on which the terrorist thrives," said Mrs. Margaret Thatcher.[43] Handling of media could spell the difference between success and failure of an operation.

Crafting Military Doctrine

The military doctrine must perforce fit into the total response system of the government. To that extent, a job sharing praxis needs to be developed at two levels: first, between the Armed Forces and the civil administration at the central, state, and local levels; and, second, between the Army, its formations, Special Forces and specialist units, elite commando units like the NSG, CPOs, and local police forces. There also has to be constant intelligence sharing amongst them. In a study of the British Army in counter-insurgency operations, David A. Charters, Director of the Centre for Conflict Studies avers that military doctrine is a body of periodically revised collective wisdom based on experience "to provide all arms and services with standardised tactical procedures".[44] That would be taking too narrow a view of the issue in the Indian context. The Army in the British system operate in a developed political system having a distinct strategic culture. The internal security adviser to the British Prime Minister is, traditionally a serving military officer. In the Indian system, the Army Chief wasn't even consulted in handling a major terrorist incident (Kandahar hijack). The military must insist on being included in the consultative process early on, and must remain fully in picture about any developing situations. Considering that effective political negotiations form the hub of sub-conventional conflict resolution, the military aim in tandem with the state's aim should be, "To create suitable conditions for negotiations favourable to the state."[45] Forces missions should be evolved within this ambit.

However, there is one question that the Armed Forces need to resolve themselves. When it comes to dealing with insurgency, the Army likes to play "reluctant good Samaritans". The currently held belief is: "The army's primary mission is to defend the country against external aggression. Its secondary task is to assist state and central governments in maintaining internal security as well as providing relief during natural calamities."[46] Indian Army's involvement with counter-insurgency is a *de facto* reality—as old as the outbreak of insurgency in the country. Lately, counter-terrorism has been added to its messy kitty. Starting with the Naga insurgency where the army was first employed in 1955, there has been no time when army has not been combating insurgency in one part of the country, or another. In fact, except for Punjab, where it played a supportive role to Punjab Police, everywhere else, counter-insurgency has primarily been an army responsibility. As for counter-terrorism, the core of the NSG, country's premier counter-terrorism force comprises two Special Action Groups, meant for very high risk specialised tasks, entirely formed of commandoes drawn from army and employed under direction of army officers. The question may be posed, "What difference would it make? The Army has always taken on assigned tasks and given a good account of itself." The answer is that today terrorism has risen to the strategic level. If it be so, how can the defence services remain aloof from it? The difference would be that the Armed Forces would raise, train, and equip units accordingly and deploy its intelligence sources with an eye on the developing insurgent and terrorist situations.

The Armed Forces (Special Powers) Act 1958 (AFSPA) gives legal authority for troops to operate in insurgency and terrorism affected areas. The Army must have the cover of this Act. In disturbed conditions, when there is a danger at every corner, the armed forces will not be able to perform counter-insurgency or counter-terrorist operations without legal authorisation of this nature.[47]

General K V Krishna Rao recommends, "On the military front, the Security Forces need to develop intelligence, understand the tactics of the insurgents, coordinate the efforts of different agencies, dominate the area effectively, maintain strict discipline among their ranks, carry out civic action to win over the people and endeavour to make themselves acceptable to the people. It must be ensured that insurgents are isolated and firmly dealt with, without alienating the population at large, whose hearts and minds must be won."[48] The recommendations represent the distilled wisdom of the Indian Army. Certain other important areas are—providing continuity—the Army is seeking it through Rashtriya Rifles (RR), a force earmarked for combating insurgency, and raising "Home and Hearth battalions"[49] —militia units now being formed in J&K from the locals and pro-active use of surrendered militants for intelligence work and hitting out at insurgents, improvement in troops mobility by using helicopters-needs to be enhanced, increased use of Mine Protected Vehicles (MPV) for safe movement along roads, training of all ranks in recognising and dealing with Improvised Explosive Devices (IED), psychological warfare, media interaction, and taking care of human rights concerns.

The Armed Forces, in addition need to develop a joint counter-terrorist capability to operate internationally and in all the environments—ground, air and marine.[50] Operation Cactus in Maldives (1988) was a tri-service operation that brought lot of credit to India. It could happen again. Entebbe was a joint operation of the IDF Army and Air Force. The Armed Forces must also prepare for WMD terrorism with inputs, technical assistance, and specialist manpower both from the defence forces and specialist civil agencies. Only the defence forces can provide the organisation and wherewithal for such an emergency.

Forecast modelling based on past experience, continuous intelligence gathering and appreciation at higher levels of command is another area that needs to be looked at. Being forewarned is being forearmed. For example, spread of Naxalite activity from Andhra Pradesh and Bihar to UP and likely spill over of Nepal's Maoist insurgency to India need to be watched with care and pro-active intelligence efforts made at this stage itself without waiting for orders from the civil authorities.

Conclusion

International terrorism has emerged as a major strategic challenge to world governments. Despite her long involvement with insurgency and spectacular acts of terrorism, India's response to sub-conventional conflict war has been amateurish, patchy and ineffectual. This would appear to be the result of absence of a "conflict management design" and scheme incorporating all agencies of the state and the nation in a coordinated whole. Sub-conventional conflict can no longer be treated as a side show. Events of 9/11 and December 2001 attack on the Indian Parliament show that the threat has already assumed strategic dimensions.

Recently the Indian Army has enunciated its doctrine for conventional war. It is only appropriate, in view of the changed threat scenario, military doctrine is enunciated for sub-conventional warfare as well taking it to be a threat of strategic dimensions. The Army's official line is: "the Army must prepare to fight along the entire spectrum of war ranging from LIC to nuclear conflict." The Army needs to prove it in practice. Presently, maximum budgetary allocations are used up in preparing for conventional war. The manpower for raising the Rashtriya Rifles is found by milking existing units. Even, armoured corps units are being employed in counter-insurgency role after shedding and moth-balling their equipment. The Army needs to correct these imbalances.

Often the term doctrine is used very loosely, alternating with such terms as, policy, strategy, military doctrine, tactical doctrine and so on. As per one view, "Doctrine is a heuristic device— a set of rules of thumb that offers a quick entry into the solution of a problem. Instead of searching its entire knowledge base each time it tackles a problem, the mind employs ready to use rules of thumb that give swift and reliable access to solutions to a common set of problems.... Nevertheless, doctrine does not provide a complete solution...only the beginning of one."[51]

No amount of experience would have prepared American people or the government for the horrors of 9/11. Once a country is struck, there is little time to think and improvise responses. One dilemma that a statesman and planner would always face is that even with the best of intelligence, it is not always possible to divine terrorist intentions for a strike like 9/11, or for that matter attack on the Indian Parliament. But reactions can certainly be made quicker and sure-footed if there is a design and doctrine in place.

References

1. Stephen M. Walt, "Beyond bin Laden: Reshaping U.S. Foreign Policy"; in Foreign Affairs — America and the World: Debating the New Shape of International Politics; (New York, Council on Foreign Relations, 2002); p. 320.
2. Brian Michael Jenkins, "Redefining Enemy— The World has Changed, But Our Mindset Has Not"; RAND Review, RAND Corporation, Santa Monica, USA, Spring 2004. Accessed at http://www.rand.org/ in December 2004.
3. B. Raman, "Terrorism: The New Context", *Strategic Analysis*, New Delhi, Vol. XXV No. 9, Dec. 2001. p. 995. Raman identifies two types of terrorism: objective terrorism to achieve certain demands, and punishment terrorism to punish the enemy.
4. Lieutenant General BS Malik (Retd.), "International Terrorism and the 'War on Terror'", Journal of the United Service Institution of India (USI Journal), New Delhi, Vol. CXXXIV, No. 558, Oct.-Dec. 2004. p. 555.
5. Amnon Barzilai, "Reinventing Warfare", HAARETZ.com; January 23, 2005. At http://www.haaretz.com accessed on January 23, 2005.
6. *Ibid.*
7. Air Commodore Jasjit Singh (Retired), *India's Defence Spending — Assessing Future Needs*; New Delhi, 2000, p. 185.
8. Major Kiran Krishan, "Armageddon"; 1977; Unpublished MS submitted to the Defence Services Staff College, Wellington, India in partial fulfillment of curriculum requirements.
9. Dan Meridor, quoted in Amnon Barzilai. n. 5.
10. K Subrahmanyam, "Organised crime & global terrorism"; *Economic Times*, New Delhi, October 9, 1997. Also see "Nuclear terrorism threat real: IAEA"; news extract from *The Hindu*, New Delhi, November 13, 2001; reproduced in *Strategic Digest*, New Delhi, January 2002. pp. 66-67.
11. Lalit Kumar/TNN, "2 held with weapons-grade uranium in Bareilly"; *Times of India*, Chandigarh, February 5, 2005.
12. "FBI nabs UK-Indian trying to sell missile to terrorists"; *Indian Express*, Chandigarh, August 14, 2003.

13. K Subrahmanyam, "Organised crime & global terrorism"; n. 10.

14. Kiran Krishan, "Mercenary or corporate executive?"; *Economic Times*, New Delhi, April 24, 2004. p. 4.

15. Thomas Friedman; quoted in Dan Meridor, "Deterrence in the Era of Terrorism and Non-Conventional Weaponry"; *Jerusalem Issue Brief*, Vol. 2, No. 2, February 9, 2003. At http://www.haaretz.com accessed in November 2004.

16. Prakash Singh, "Manmohan Singh, beware of becoming a softie — An open Letter to Prime Minister of India"; *Indian Express*, Chandigarh, January 26, 2005. p. 9. Prakash Singh is a former Director General of Border Security Force. Also see Kanti P. Bajpai, "The Roots of Terrorism"; In Derek O' Brien Ed., *The Penguin India Yearbook* 2005; (New Delhi, Penguin Books, 2005). Pp. 684-685.

17. Samudra Gupta Kashyap, "A militant haven"; *Indian Express*, Chandigarh, December 6, 2004. p. 9.

18. Nadeem Ahmed, "Naxalism refuses to die in India"; *HindustanTimes.com Special*, June 7, 2003, at http://www.hindustantimes.com/news/6253_249850,0009.htm, accessed on January 27, 2005.

19. Ajai Sahni, quoted in Arun Shourie, "Listening to Sufi music as thousands are murdered — India under threat Part-I"; *Indian Express*, Chandigarh, December 15, 2004. p. 9.

20. P. C. Alexander, quoted in "Teflon Generals"; Editorial; *Hindustan Times*, Chandigarh, September 16, 2004. p. 8.

21. Brahma Chellany, "Anniversary of shame"; *Hindustan Times*, Chandigarh, December 31, 2004. p. 8.

22. General Shankar Roy Chowdhury quoted in news item, "Op Parakram was a disaster"; *Hindustan Times*, Chandigarh, December 9, 2003. p. 10. Also see, Brig Kiran Krishan, "US polls: Security lessons for us"; *Hindustan Times*, Chandigarh, November 11, 2004. p. 9; and news item, "CCS puts hot pursuit, air strikes on hold"; *Hindustan Times*, Chandigarh, December 18, 2001 The Cabinet Committee on Security (CCS) was briefed at the Prime Minister's residence by the defence services chiefs on December 17, 2001. They had reportedly advised covert action alongside a politico-military

offensive. Only history would reveal how deep and effective the consultation process was. Cut and dried briefings could hardly substitute policy and doctrinal guidelines, and continuous and institutionalised consultations on a regular basis.

23. Jaswant Singh, *Defending India*; (New Delhi, Macmillan, 1999): p. 270.
24. K P S Gill. Punjab: *The Knights of Falsehood*; New Delhi, Har-Anand Publications, 1997; p. 10.
25. *Ibid.*
26. Lieutenant Colonel S P Anand, "Counter-Insurgency Theory and Practice in Mizo Hills"; *USI Journal*, Vol. CI, No. 423, April-June 1971. pp. 150-56.
27. General V P Malik (Retd.); In conversation with the writer at Panchkula on January 5, 2005.
28. Vishal Thapar, "PM explains move to defence brass"; *Sunday Hindustan Times*, November 2, 2003. p. 1. Also see Atal Behari Vajpayee, "Shrug off the Cold War, this is a new World"; *Indian Express*, Chandigarh, November 7, 2003. p. 9.
29. General K V Krishna Rao (Retd), "Insurgency in the North East — Part I"; *USI Journal*, New Delhi, Vol. CXXVIII, No. 531, Jan.-March 1998. p. 13.
30. Government of India, "Report of the Group of Ministers on Internal Security"; February 19, 2001, Chapter IV, pp. 41-57.
31. *Ibid.* p. 51.
32. Kuldip Nayar, "Rebels, not criminals"; *Indian Express*, Chandigarh, January 4, 2205. p. 8.
33. Noam Chomsky, For Reasons of State; (New Delhi, *Penguin*, 2003, First published in 1972 by *Pantheon Books*, USA); p. 212.
34. Arun Shourie, "Responding to Terrorism"; In K P S Gill & Ajai Sahni Eds., *The Global Threat of Terror — Ideological, Material and Political Linkages*; (New Delhi, Roli books & Institute For Conflict Management, 2003); pp. 18-19.
35. Tribune News Service, "Army chief for humane touch to anti-terror drive"; *The Tribune*, Chandigarh, February 2, 2005.

p. 1. Also see Rajat Pandit/TNN, "The 'humane face of Indian Army — JJ Singh For Winning Hearts And Minds"; *Times of India*, Chandigarh, February 2, 2005. p. 1; and, Vishal Thapar, "No more 'kills' orders JJ"; *Hindustan Times*; Chandigarh, February 2, 2005. p. 7.

36. Hans Morgenthau (1973), "Six Principles of Political Realism"; In Lawrence Freedman, Ed., *War*; (New York, Oxford University Press, 1994); p. 160-161.

37. Thomas Schelling (1963), "The Strategy of Conflict"; In Lawrence Freedman, Ed., *War*; (New York, Oxford University Press, 1994); p. 205.

38. Richard K Betts (1994), quoted in Rajat Ganguly & Ian Macduff Eds., *Ethnic Conflict and Secessionism in South Asia and Southeast Asia — Causes, Dynamics*, Solutions; (New Delhi, Sage Publications, 2003); p. 18.

39. D. G. Pruitt and J. Z. Rubin, quoted in Rajat Ganguly & Ian Macduff Eds., *ibid.* p. 18.

40. Bibhu Prasad Routray, "ULFA: Playing Hard to Get"; *South Asia Intelligence Review (SAIR)*, Vol.3, No. 22, December 13, 2004; South Asia Terrorism Portal at http://www.satp.org.

41. *Ibid.* n. 40.

42. Sultan Shahin, "Tangled roots in India's border conflicts"; *Asia Times*, May 5, 2001. At http://www.atimes.com/atimes.

43. Quoted in Arun Shourie, *op. cit.*, n. 34. p. 19.

44. David A. Charters, "From Palestine to Northern Ireland: British Adaptation to Low-intensity Operations"; In David A. Charters and Maurice Tugwell Eds., *Armies in Low-Intensity Conflict: A Comparative Analysis*; (London & Toronto, Brassey's, 1989); p. 230.

45. *GoM Report.* n. 30. Para 4.3 p. 41.

46. Ashok K. Mehta, "Cleaning up the mess"; *Hindustan Times*, Chandigarh, March 14, 2002. p. 8.

47. General V P Malik (Retd.), "Act of last resort — Don't blame Manipur's problems on the Armed Forces (Special Powers) Act. At http://www.orfonline.org/analysis on November 17, 2004.

48. General K V Krishna Rao (Retd.), "Insurgency in the North East — Part I"; *USI Journal,* Vol. CXXVIII, No. 531, January-March 1998. pp. 10-25.
49. Also see General V P Malik, "Security on the borderline"; *Indian Express,* Chandigarh, September 18, 2004. p. 8.
50. General V P Malik (Retd.), "Maritime counter-terrorism — Army has a crucial role to play"; *The Tribune,* Chandigarh, January 1, 2005, p. 10.
51. Robert R. Leonhard, *The Principles of War for the Information Age;* (Novato, California, USA, Presidio Press, 1998); pp. xiv-xv.

Index